# The Paper Republic Guide to Contemporary Chinese Literature

纸·托·邦

CHINESE LITERATURE
IN TRANSLATION

2021 · London · Seattle

Paper Republic is a registered charity in the UK,
charity number 1182259

25 Park Avenue
Chelmsford, CM1 2AB
UK

ISBN: 978-1-3999-1054-5

Layout and design by Andy Zhou, Jiangyue Qiu

# *Contents*

# PREFACE

What is a guide, but an aid to a visitor to an unfamiliar land? The 'unfamiliar land' in this case is Chinese literature, in its English translation; the visitor is the curious reader; and the guide is this one: the *Paper Republic Guide to Contemporary Chinese Literature*.

Paper Republic was founded by a group of translators in Beijing in 2007 as an online forum. It is now a non-profit, registered as a charity in the UK and with a global reach. The organization is independent, and is run by volunteers who, between them, have a fund of knowledge about contemporary Chinese writers and translation. Our goals are to tell readers what's good and available to read, and to encourage the highest standards of literary translation. In short, we identify the very best new Chinese writing – and promote it in translation to the English-speaking world. In recent years, the field of translated Chinese fiction has begun to blossom, both in the number of translations and in the diversity of information sources. Which is where the *Paper Republic Guide to Contemporary Chinese Literature* comes in.

To help guide an interested reader, we have asked six writers to reflect on various themes and topics. In the introduction to the *Guide*, Xiaolu Guo looks back to her youth and how different authors influenced her writing life. Dylan Levi King examines the social and political roles Chinese authors have taken on since the May Fourth Movement of 1919, which marked the beginning of modern Chinese literature. Others write about genres they favor or have followed in the past. Emily Xueni Jin traces the development of Chinese science fiction and its place in the global world of science fiction. Rachel Cheung takes the reader into the online world of internet fiction that once captivated her. Ping Zhu takes a scholarly and sober look at women's writing as part of gender consciousness, while Andrea Lingenfelter leads us on a whirlwind tour of writings from Hong Kong. Each writer comes from a different background, and their contributions, together with the descriptions of the authors listed in the *Guide*, provide fascinating insights into contemporary Chinese literature.

These essays are supplemented by the directory of authors and publications in the second half of the *Guide*. Any document claiming to be a guide ought to state its criteria for what it has included and excluded – first and most simply, we included any author mentioned by name by our essayists. Beyond that, we focussed on still-living Sinophone writers with publications in English, who have been active since the end of the Cultural Revolution, with a slight leaning towards Mainland China (for no other reason than the limits of our own knowledge), and with special dispensation given for a few major historical figures such as Eileen Chang and Lu Xun.

We offer this limited slice of the full spectrum of Chinese literature in anticipation of future editions of the *Guide*, which we hope will expand in scope even as the field of Chinese literature in translation burgeons.

We are painfully aware that there are many other excellent authors who, for reasons of space, we have been unable to include. Please go to our website and database, Paper-Republic.org (https://paper-republic.org/), for a more comprehensive selection. In the meantime we sincerely hope that you, the reader, with the benefit of this edition, will find this 'land' less unfamiliar, and be prepared to strike out into it unaided.

Eric Abrahamsen and Yvette Zhu

All members of the Paper Republic team worked on the *Guide*. At the time of writing, they were:

**Eric Abrahamsen**
Translator, publishing consultant and founder of Paper Republic. Eric is our Chair of Trustees.

**Nicky Harman**
Translator, educator and blogger.

**Emily Jones**
Translator, and consultant in brand and marketing

**Jack Hargreaves**
Translator

**Yvette Zhu**
Translator and author

**Yao Lirong**
Translator and Beijing correspondent

**Dylan Levi King**
Translator

Special thanks go to

**Ms Yuan Shuang**
Focal Point for Nanjing UNESCO
Creative City of Literature and
Director of Nanjing Literature
Centre, for a generous donation

**Duncan Hewitt**
Journalist and translator, for
proof-reading and editorial advice

**Dr Amy Mathewson**
for help with copy-editing

**Bai Liye**
senior advisor for the Nanjing
literature centre, for help with
copy-editing.

And to the volunteers who wrote many of the author
biographies, without whom we could not have completed
the project.

They are:

Fenella Barber (FB)
Aoife Cantrill (AC)
Renée Elizabeth Clark (REC)
Markéta Glanzová (MG)
Anna Gustafson (AG)

Terezia Hegerová (TH)
Mavis Lee (ML)
Bingbing Shi (BBS)
Catherine Xin Xin Yu (CXXY)

For further details about our volunteers, please see:
https://paper-republic.org/about/support-us/

All unattributed biographies were written by members of
the Paper Republic team.

# CONTRIBUTORS

Rachel Cheung is a writer based in Hong Kong. She reports on art, culture and social topics relevant to the region. She has contributed to live coverage of the protest movement in Hong Kong as well as covering major cultural events. Her work has appeared in the *Los Angeles Times*, the *Washington Post* and the *World Politics Review*, among other news outlets.

Xiaolu Guo is a writer and film-maker. Her novels include *A Concise Chinese–English Dictionary for Lovers*, shortlisted for the 2007 Orange Prize for Fiction. Her memoir *Nine Continents* received the National Book Critics Circle Award in 2017. Her recent novel *A Lover's Discourse* was published by Grove Atlantic in 2020, and was shortlisted for the Goldsmith Prize. She has also directed feature films including *She, A Chinese* and won the Golden Leopard at the Locarno Film Festival 2009. She lives in Berlin and London.

Emily Xueni Jin is a science fiction and fantasy translator, translating between Chinese and English in both directions. She graduated from Wellesley College in 2017, and she is currently pursuing a PhD in East Asian Languages and Literature at Yale University.

Dylan Levi King is a Tokyo-based writer and translator. His most recent translation is Cai Chongda's *Vessel* (HarperCollins).

Andrea Lingenfelter is a poet, scholar of Chinese literature, and the translator of *The Changing Room: Selected Poetry of Zhai Yongming* (Northern California Book Award); Hon Lai Chu's *The Kite Family* (NEA Translation Fellowship); Li Pik-wah's *Farewell My Concubine* and *The Last Princess of Manchuria*; *Candy and Vanishing Act* by Mian Mian; and *Ghosts City Sea* – poems by Wang Yin. Her work has appeared in the *Los Angeles Review of Books*, *Manoa*, *Granta*, *Washington Square Review*, *Chinese Literature Today*, *Pathlight*, *Words Without Borders*, *Asian CHA*, and *Two Lines*. She teaches literary translation and Asia Pacific literature and film at the University of San Francisco.

Ping Zhu is an associate professor of Chinese Literature at the University of Oklahoma and serves as the acting editor-in-chief of *Chinese Literature Today*. She is the author of *Gender and Subjectivities in Early Twentieth-century Chinese Literature and Culture* (Palgrave, 2015), the co-editor (with Zhuoyi Wang and Jason McGrath) of *Maoist Laughter* (Hong Kong University Press, 2019), which won Choice's Outstanding Academic Title in 2020, and the co-editor (with Hui Faye Xiao) of *Feminisms with Chinese Characteristics* (Syracuse University Press, 2021).

# INTRODUCTION

*Exceedingly Loud and Incredibly Quiet*

'The world is yours, as well as ours, but in the last analysis, it is yours. You young people, full of vigor and vitality, are in the bloom of life, like the sun at eight or nine in the morning. Our hope is placed on you. The world belongs to you. China's future belongs to you.'

Mao's slogan was still ringing in my ears as I entered the university in September 1993 for the first time. I was barely 20, but I had the ears of an 80 year old. I guess not only me. In those days, many young people could recite those lines, even if they were self-styled punk youth.

In the same week, I was reading a translation of Sylvia Plath's poetry. I was captivated by passages such as: 'Dying is an art, like everything else. I do it exceptionally well. I do it so it feels like hell. I do it so it feels real. I guess you could say I've a call.' And then another poem titled 'Daddy': 'Every woman adores a Fascist, The boot in the face, the brute.'

It felt to me that however loud and important Mao's speech was supposed to be, these lines sounded much louder. Exceedingly loud and shockingly private. But at the same time, they were incredibly quiet. This poetry was quiet because it was private. It would never ever be broadcast in our schoolyard with its loud speakers blasting in every direction. Dying is an art, like everything else. Sure, I understood that. But – 'I do it exceptionally well' - I was not sure what Plath meant. Then the less obscure lines 'Every woman adores a Fascist...', I could see that very well. It was clear. Wasn't it? I loved that kind of literature. So I told myself: if I could write that kind of poetry, a private and personal one, the opposite of Mao's, I would be pleased. I would feel that I managed to achieve something unique, even with a boot in my face.

So in the following years, with the sounds of Beijing's most intense period of urban construction continuously rumbling around me, I wrote one novel after another in a similar manner – quiet and private. First was *Twenty Fragments of a Ravenous Youth*, then *Village of Stone*. Since I was allergic to a certain post-revolutionary language, I wrote my books in the borrowed styles of Western authors: Plath, Joyce, Calvino, Borges, Woolf, Beckett, and Duras. Always in the first person voice, monologues, no history, no plots, no traditional beginning or ending. At the same time, I was looking around, searching for a familiar language that I could naturally connect to. Then I discovered two Chinese writers: Liu Suola and Chen Ran. They were Beijing-based, both were in their 30s and wonderfully attractive to my young eyes. Their style (defined as avant-garde in the 1990s) was the most direct influence on my early writing.

I had had some naïve belief that an interesting writer should also be a *Lebenskünstler*, a life artist. Liu Suola was a Renaissance woman who fitted my idea of a modern artist. She was a composer and musician, a graduate of the Central Conservatory of Music in Beijing. Since the 1980s, she has never stopped writing novels and performing her music on stage. Liu's novels are a verbal symphony of impressive staccato and scherzo movements. Her debut novel *You Have No Choice*, is about young musicians in an art academy and how they confront a traditional collective society. After I read the novel, I suddenly became aware that I was 'an individual' with a different identity from others, especially from older generations. Of course I had that awareness from reading Duras and Salinger. But Western voices seem to be rooted in individuality and singularity. It was difficult to turn their voices into mine. But Liu Suola's prose resonated with my reality as a young artist in the 1990s. I was studying at the Beijing Film Academy and dreamt of becoming a new Eisenstein or a female Godard. Alone and away from my home province, I was surrounded by underground artists, including the soon-to-be world-renowned filmmakers of the Sixth Generation. I saw how my classmate Jia Zhangke made his first short film before he conquered the Cannes Film Festival, and I collaborated on a screenplay with Wang Xiaoshuai before he won awards at Cannes and the Berlin Film Festival. One thing was for sure: you had to learn to shout or scream with big lungs in a society like that. All of Liu Suola's novels were loud individual statements, yet delicate and risky, for that sort of voice could be easily muffled by the state censorship of the time.

Even though the trauma of the Cultural Revolution seemed to have been deflected by economic forces in the 1990s and early 2000s, any stylistic voices about private lives were still viewed as 'negative' by patriarchal critical establishments in China. If your preference (such as mine) was to read interior, private narratives, you often had to go back to the pre-Mao era. To Eileen Chang and Lu Xun, and earlier still, to the folklores and dramas of the Ming and Qing Dynasties, or the love poetry of the Tang and Song Dynasties. But in 1996, in one of the Sanlitun cafés, I read Chen Ran's *Private Life*. I was immediately taken with her prose. She wrote nothing grand or serious, but every sentence revealed a naked honesty and a unique femininity. Her self-reflective manner and seemingly very quiet world suggested a true modernity to me. To encounter her work was so inspirational for me. I had been stuck in the mud of translated Western work, or repetitive Chinese family sagas from state writers. How many sweeping family sagas could I take, I asked myself? One is enough, ten is suffocating. Chen Ran's work suggested a beautiful quietness and interiority which I could only encounter in the works of Duras or Calvino. And in real life, in Beijing at the time, the concept of 'cool' replaced the word 'modern' for performance artists and newly emerging punk rock musicians. Writers seemed to be the last group to be cool, at least from a superficial glance. But just look at the author's photo published on the back of Chen Ran's novels, that was definitely what 'cool' was meant to be. In the headshot, she had an alluring expression. One side of her hair was shaved up above her ear, the other side long and soft. She was a real punk (in a mysterious manner, the opposite of Liu Suola's style).

But just like Liu, in my eyes, Chen was an embodiment of artistic cool. I thought to myself then: wouldn't it be great if I could write and live like that? To lead a private and artistic life, away from ideology.

By the time my own novels were published in the late 1990s, I confronted similar critiques to those that Chen Ran and Liu Suola had faced. The mainstream critics, especially the male academics, accused me of narcissism (*zilian*) and anti-socialness (*zibi*). These negative views were also directed towards writers such as Mian Mian and Wei Hui, two women writers based in Shanghai who had caused a sensation with their narratives about drugs and sex. I wondered, if we were considered narcissistic and anti-social, what would they make of Rimbaud, Baudelaire, Woolf and indeed, Plath? Do we need to change society in order to alter the opinions of the powerful literary pundits? Are we supposed to believe that reflecting on a personal life is mere exhibitionism? Even worse, should we still surrender to the idea put so forcefully by the character of the commissar Strelnikov in *Doctor Zhivago*: 'The personal life is dead in Russia, history has killed it.' So was that it? There was no resurrection of personal life in the most populated country in the world?

Even if history had killed the personal life, writers like Bei Dao, Yang Lian, Yu Hua, Zhu Wen, Wang Anyi, Hong Ying, Alai, and so on have managed to recover personal lives from the ashes of collective memory. So have artists from other media, such as cinema, visual art, music etc.

It was during that period of complex social changes that I became immersed in the works of Wang Shuo, Tie Ning, Su Tong and Chi Zijian, and revisited older generation authors such as Mo Yan, Wang Meng, Jia Pingwa, Liu Heng, and Yan Lianke. Obviously, sweeping historical gestures are more pronounced in the novels of older generation authors. Their narratives rooted in the tradition of agricultural life directly reflect the trauma of the Mao era. Some of these works have been successfully adapted into epic films that reached international film festivals. Films based on novels like Mo Yan's *Red Sorgum*, Ah Cheng's *King of Children*, Li Bihua's *Farewell My Concubine*, Yu Hua's *To Live*, Bai Xianyong's *Taipei People*, and many more. As a result, they effectively promoted Chinese literature to the Western world.

But how should Westerners read contemporary Chinese literature? Where to start? What are the most accessible forms? Before I came to the West, I never considered 'the novel' – a medium book-sized 300 page narrative paperback – as a central literary form. I felt that the standard novel format has been a sort of commodity, an industrial mainstream product. The forms I was used to (perhaps this is even more the case for older generations) were short stories, essays, and poems. Very often, you could grab some newspaper or magazine in the street and read a beautiful essay in a column by a well-known author. But that sort of spontaneous prose had disappeared. Looking back into the past, there were many wonderful texts written in that manner. Lu Xun is a perfect example. His essays are masterpieces of the last century. They are short and concise, each is like the punch of a fist, but the blow is softened by reflective memory. His short stories such as *A Madman's Diary* and *The True Story of Ah Q* were powerful antidotes to social ills. They were short, originally published in newspapers and magazines, and were not aimed at garnering literary prizes or status. Such forms, once a vital part of street life and public discourse, can now appear in the virtual domain of the iPhone and the internet (though its objectivity needs to be questioned).

I still have a problem with calling a writer a novelist. 'Novelist' suggests a certain limitation imposed by the current consumer-driven publishing industry. Some of my favourite Chinese writers were at the same time intellectuals and filmmakers. Zhu Wen is a great example. His short stories have a distinctive satirical style just like his independently-produced underground films. Since the 1980s, novelists and sociologists such as Wang Xiaobo and Li Yinghe initiated a strong social debate about gender and sexualities in China. Poet and filmmaker Yin Lichuan, blogger Murong Xuexun, writer Fang Fang and so on belong to the era when literature has become embedded in social media and other forms of expression subject to state approval. Indeed, every writer is, or should be, a poet, a social commentator and a public intellectual. These are essential to the nature of writing and being an author and cannot be ignored when we talk about contemporary Chinese literature.

So far we have been looking at the recent past. But I would like to use this introduction also to anticipate future trends. To really grasp all that's going on in contemporary Chinese literature we need a new lexicon. We are living in the time of multilingualism and mass migration. The idea of 'national literature' gives us a picture of writing confined to islands, a cultural essence that is fixed, tribal, and immobile. With multilingual and transnational identities having become state-of-the-art with the new generation, we cannot continue this kind of lazy labelling. We have to ask ourselves in what sense there is Chinese Literature rather than a literature of a multitude of voices variously engaged with China. Being inclusive is always wiser than being exclusive. If we do pay attention to writers from Taiwan, Hong Kong, Tibet, Xinjiang, and indeed, from overseas, migrant as well as the exiled writers, then we can release ourselves from the imprisoning concept of 'national literature' and its false identity. This in turn allows us to introduce readers to a much wider and diverse literary territory. After all, reading is about encountering and engaging with the other. Through diverse reading, we are able to uncover the hidden memories of Chinese labourers immersed in the sugar cane fields of Cuba or in the goldmines of Ghana. We meet Ha Jin in Boston and Gao Xingjian in Paris. And we should also be joyful that these writers are not satisfied with delivering China-only subjects. Shan Sa lives in France and writes in French, her topics range from the 1989 Tiananmen Movement to European history; Ma Jian lives in Britain and writes about China in all sorts of real and surreal ways, yet he is a monolingual writer in a traditional sense. The same goes for Liao Yiwu. Liao is exiled in Germany but offers some of the most honest and painful accounts of Chinese society. Then there are those international voices with Chinese roots, who bear double identities linguistically and culturally, such as Amy Tan and Qiu Xiaolong, Jung Chang and Yan Geling. Not to mention the forthcoming generation of new Chinese writers, the ones I have taught in Columbia University and the City University of New York. Some of these Chinese students even write in their third language, and their stories have amazed me. To me, the 'outcast' writers who are manifestly Chinese but refuse to be defined by a single language and nationality can offer us very exciting literary dialogues. These outsiders' transnational qualities truly bridge the still deep chasm between the East and West.

For the same reasons, I believe translators and transnational writers are crucial to building dialogue between divided worlds. One of my favourite lines from *Four Quartets* by T. S. Eliot is: 'For last year's words belong to last year's language. And next year's words await another voice.' Obviously, T. S. Eliot speaks much more clearly than I do about the ever-changing character of literary identities. I am therefore borrowing T. S. Eliot to express my deep gratitude to the translators who have devoted their time and energy in bringing Chinese literature to the world, and in particular, the translators and editors of this book, *The Guide to Contemporary Chinese Literature*. I believe that its scope will expand each year as our horizon expands, allowing us to wonder at the discovery of the unknown.

Xiaolu Guo, London, October 2020

# The Role of *the Author in China*

Dylan Levi King

In China, books are considered worth banning because the ideas they contain are powerful. From the birth of modern Chinese literature in the New Culture Movement of the early 20th century, writers staked out a role as polemicists and social critics – even the choice to write in an accessible vernacular language was a political decision. Chairman Mao was careful to lay out rules for writers at the Yan'an Forum in 1942, emphasizing that art should serve politics. The Cultural Revolution was started indirectly by a squabble over a play. The Anti-Spiritual Pollution Campaign of the 1980s took aim at writers for promoting humanism and existentialism. The Nationalist government in Taiwan banned most of the writers celebrated on the Mainland, including Lu Xun. Writers wield the power of literature and therefore have obligations – in China, to even attempt to deny that could be seen as inflammatory.

This belief in the political power of literature has led to the dominance of certain literary forms. In the West, the long tradition of social novels is mostly seen as a relic of the past. But modern Chinese literature remains deeply influenced by the realist writers of the 19th century – Charles Dickens, Thomas Hardy, Ivan Turgenev, and Honoré de Balzac – whose hold over Western literature has weakened. Postmodern literature and discourse emerged in China in the 1990s but has never threatened the supremacy of social realism. Whereas it would be unthinkable for a contemporary American writer to produce a sincere update of Harriet Beecher Stowe's *Uncle Tom's Cabin* or Upton Sinclair's *The Jungle*, these forms are still popular with Chinese writers. The modern Chinese novel usually carries an explicit social critique or ideological message – and the absence of a critique or message is often seen as a major failing by the literary establishment, bureaucratic busybodies, state newspaper op-ed writers, as well as critics and readers. Wei Hui's *Shanghai Baby*, for example, a novel about a Shanghai waitress juggling affairs, is rarely criticized for the quality of the writing but for its ideological failings.

Perhaps the best way to get at what being a writer has meant and might now mean in contemporary Chinese society is to pull a few names out of the pantheon and figure out why their busts are on the mantle.

We can start with Lu Xun (1881–1936). Everyone starts with Lu Xun – with good reason. A democratizer of language, Lu Xun was considered one of the early masters of the vernacular, rather than the classical style that was used to compose the most serious literature in China up until the early 20th century. More than the literary quality of his work, Lu Xun has remained important for the message of national salvation that he brought to the masses. Literature was seen by Lu Xun and his peers as a tool to address injustices. Writers and intellectuals in China were deeply involved in the project of rebuilding the nation in the 20th century and Lu Xun is the model of the author as national conscience, and of the author as instructor.

Eileen Chang (a.k.a. Zhang Ailing, 1920–1995), on the other hand, is remembered for the beauty of her writing, for her genius, and for her meditations on human nature. Liu Zaifu (1941– ), one of the preeminent thinkers on modern Chinese literature, called Eileen Chang one of the most important philosophical writers. He writes, 'She sees a wilderness where other people see civilization, the powerlessness of human emotion where other people see emotional strength, and possibilities where other people see impossibilities.' Reading Eileen Chang is an aesthetic and emotional pleasure and she is rarely – in her better work, at least – didactic. But it is precisely because she defied any political labels, and seemed uninterested in engaging directly with the rebuilding of the nation, that Eileen Chang was so long denied her place in the history of Chinese literature by critics and academics who wrote her off as a lightweight. Eileen Chang is the chronicler of minor human tragedy, and was seen as a conceited, self-romanticizing aesthete.

It is debatable whether or not Hao Ran (1932–2008) would actually have a bust on the mantlepiece of 20th century Chinese literature, but I am using him here as a stand-in for the now mostly-forgotten writers who answered the call of the Party. Hao Ran came from a peasant family and got his start as an author by writing a skit for a district Party committee event. He climbed his way through literary bureaucracy and eventually earned a job editing a Party journal. He is often remembered for his statement that he was not a writer at all, but rather a 'full-time worker in the field of literature and art.' There is a misconception that Chinese literature of the Maoist period was marching in lockstep with Soviet literary theory. In fact, writer-theoreticians like Hao Ran – following the direction of the Chairman and other top leaders, of course – were debating, formulating, and putting into practice new ideas. The home-grown literary theories of 'revolutionary realism' and 'revolutionary romanticism' were a step beyond what was practiced in Soviet literature: they built on ideas from the May Fourth Movement of 1919, on Mao's belief that culture had far more power than Marxist-Leninist intellectuals would credit it with, and also on a desire on the part of the leadership to break away from their Russian big brother. Writing with all the required revolutionary heroics and Maoist symbolism, Hao Ran was one of the few authors in China allowed to publish new work during the Cultural Revolution. Despite his passion for the project of Chinese socialism and his position in the literary bureaucracy, Hao Ran was occasionally at odds with the leadership for perceived ideological errors in his work. This meant that some of his works appeared in dramatically different forms over the years, the result of extensive rewriting to keep up with developments in literary and political theories. He cleaved closely enough to the official line, but careful reading gives a more nuanced impression. When he wrote about, say, land reforms, he was speaking from personal experience and observations in the countryside. Hao Ran is the model of the author as part-time bureaucrat, part-time cultural worker, and occasional – perhaps unintentional – critic, and of the author as rural artist, wedded to the rustic masses and the soil.

And a fourth model: Wang Shuo (1958– ). A Beijing writer who roared to nationwide fame in 1987, he gives us another perspective on the role of the author. He was not a revolutionary or didactic writer; he never wrote on theory or ideology; it's tough to call him either a supporter or critic of the government; and there's none of Eileen Chang's purity in him. He wrote what Geremie Barmé calls 'a literature of escape and sublimation.' Wang Shuo belonged to the first generation of writers who could – and were at least superficially encouraged to – disengage from politics, enjoy the benefits of a new cultural permissiveness, and make a ton of money doing it. As he remarked in an interview: 'If you think I should be doing something for others... I reckon about the only thing I could manage to do in that department is to polish their shoes'*. Does Wang Shuo as entrepreneur undermine the central thesis that literature in China is deadly important? Maybe so; maybe not. Wang Shuo, who has published little over the past decade or so, might be remembered for his churlish TV interviews and bratty behavior, but he's also been studied, discussed at all levels of society, hotly debated, and theorized about. You can't say he's not taken seriously – even if he claims not to take himself that seriously. Wang Shuo is our author as

---

\* Translated by Gérémie Barmé in *In the Red: On Contemporary Chinese Culture* (Columbia University Press, 1999)

outsider, whose stance of cynical irony is partially his own invention, partially a result of being shut out of politics.

I present these four models as a sort of spectrum, providing, I hope, a way of understanding the role of the author – past, present, and even future.

An example: Yan Lianke's didactic, horrifying stories of modern life make for an easy comparison to Lu Xun, but understanding his delicate position in institutional literature – at once inside and outside the system – requires knowing figures like Hao Ran. Meanwhile, Chu T'ien-wen's florid language and her focus on the quiet cruelties of modern life have earned her comparisons to Eileen Chang, but, like Wang Shuo, she is a cultural entrepreneur who has worked in multiple media.

Some writers, of course, fit less neatly into this heuristic model. I am thinking of Can Xue (1953– ) and her *sui generis* experimental fiction, her pure dedication to literature, and her seeming unwillingness to play along with the rules of the establishment. I am thinking of Zhang Chengzhi (1948– ), who liberated himself from the literary bureaucracy in the 1980s, decamped to Japan, and pursued a suddenly outmoded project of global liberation, writing about Che Guevara, Japanese ultra-leftist terrorists, and international Islam, and donated the proceeds of a novel to Palestinian refugees. I am thinking about Guo Jingming (1983– ), the well-compensated, hedonistic author of online escapist urban fantasy and other genres usually deemed outside the bounds of serious literature.

Even if a writer doesn't fit neatly into one of these models, it can still be used to explain the reactions that they can expect to receive. A 2015 *China Daily* story on Guo Jingming, for example, was headlined 'Guo doesn't care.' The story quoted a film critic named Li Xingwen, who accused Guo of promoting 'vanity and material desires, not the self-claimed theme of true friendship.' This criticism of Guo Jingming's hedonism is hard to understand without knowing something of the roles authors are expected to fulfil in China.

The life-and-death stakes of Chinese literature can be hard for writers to bear. Many fine writers have had their best work banned or suppressed, or have been forced to publish it overseas. One wonders how many great works have been held back and consigned to collections of unpublishable 'desk-drawer literature' (抽屉文学) over the decades. In digital times, this is more likely to circulate among Douban contacts, for example, than be consigned to a drawer. Nevertheless, compared with the West, where literature has continuously slipped in importance, there's something almost heartening about the continuously charged significance of Chinese literature.

# Women's Writing

Ping Zhu

For centuries, "women's writing" was an unimaginable concept for the Chinese – the Confucian teachings discouraged women's learning, regarding it antagonistic to their prescribed gender roles of being virtuous wives and good mothers. The Chinese political system and cultural hierarchy perpetuated themselves partially by suppressing women's independent thinking, voices, and actions, making women subordinate to patriarchal domination. Chinese women's writing emerged from the horizon of history and became socially accepted only about a hundred years ago, when China started to embrace Western modernity amidst a deep national crisis. During the early twentieth century, women's sexuality and independence became favored literary themes, and new social roles for women were being imagined. The socialist regime (1949–1978) pushed women's liberation to an unprecedented degree by promoting women's participation in social production and guaranteeing women's equal rights with men. The gender revolution was part and parcel of modern Chinese revolutions throughout the twentieth century, and women's writing was an important gauge of the gender revolution.

Chinese women writers since the modern period have been fighting a two-front war: on the one hand, they have challenged the traditional gender roles that still subjugate women to masculine desire in its various insidious forms; on the other hand, they have questioned the socialist gender practice that purported to have erased gender differences.

In mainland China, male intellectuals regained the power of narrating history after the Cultural Revolution (1966–1976) and quickly bid farewell to the socialist legacy, including the tenet of gender equality. As a result, sexism and gender stereotypes once again abound in literary works by contemporary Chinese writers. This drastic turn of history was documented, sometimes endorsed, and sometimes challenged in women writers' literary works, which emerged as alternative historical narratives that are indispensable to the understanding of modern China. What readers will encounter in those literary works is far more than tales of victimhood, but a vibrant and colorful literary world that encompasses renewed quests for gender equality and justice, artistic portrayals of everyday minutia, candid explorations of women's sexuality and psychology, sober reflections of historical violence, and avant-gardist representations of historical trauma. Among contemporary Chinese women writers, Wang Anyi's exuberant and delectable stories, from *Song of Everlasting Sorrow*, *Fu Ping*, to *Scent of Heaven*, have depicted Shanghai and China as communities of ordinary folks, and offer sober reflections on the contemporary world. Can Xue, in contrast, has crafted surrealistic and sometimes grotesque stories (e.g., "Yellow Mud Street" and "The Hut on the Mountain") that are reminiscent of Franz Kafka's writings. Whether her stories are an allusion to the punishing regime of socialist China is open to debate, but Can Xue's later novels, such as *The Last Lover* and *Frontier*, have shed all constraints of reality and entered enchanting dreamworlds. Representative novels by other mainland Chinese women writers, such as Zhang Kangkang's *The Invisible Companion*, Tie Ning's *The Bathing Woman*, Fang Fang's *Soft Burial*, and Xu Xiaobin's *Feathered Serpent* and *Crystal Wedding*, have formed a concerted effort to weave a complex tapestry of China and the Chinese people in the late half of the twentieth century. Compared with the spellbinding autobiographies or historical novels by the group of diasporic Chinese women writers, including Jung Chang, Anchee Min, Yan Geling, and Hong Ying, the mainland Chinese women writers' works are characterized by a consistent effort to transcend sufferings through philosophical musings as well as by their relentless questioning of the self, of gender relationships, of human nature, and of women's place in history.

While some mainland Chinese women writers offer alternative narratives of history, others grapple with the gender issue. Because the popular socialist slogan "women hold up half the sky" came off as a rejection of gender differences in some people's eyes, the reclaiming of gender became a popular literary motif during the post-Mao period.* Zhang Jie is one of the first mainland Chinese women writers who voiced the existential crisis of women in the aftermath of socialist China (see Zhang's collection

---

\* Mao Zedong died in 1976.

of stories *Love Must Not Be Forgotten*). A few of Wang Anyi's early stories (*Love on a Barren Mountain*, *Love in a Small Town*, and *Brocade Valley*) indicate that she was also in a quandary about how "gender equality" should have been conceived in various situations. Chinese women's emotional and sexual awakenings during the post-Mao period were often accompanied by withdrawing of the feminine self from the social realm into the protagonist's inner world. This is vividly revealed in Lin Bai's *A War of One's Own* and Chen Ran's *A Private Life*. Since the 1990s, however, the sweeping force of the market economy has commercialized and codified the feminine consciousness and the female body, as shown by the narcissistic female characters in Wei Hui's *Shanghai Baby* and Mian Mian's *Candy*.

In recent years, Chinese women's writing is beginning to intersect with literature about, and predominantly produced by, marginalized social groups, as an increasing amount of works depicting peasants' and migrant workers' lives, feelings, and bodies have gained international visibility. Among them, Sheng Keyi, a writer known for her intense language and underlying humor, portrays the dangerous adventures of female migrant workers in her novel *Northern Girls*. Zheng Xiaoqiong is a migrant worker as well as a poet; her verses combine traditional Chinese aesthetics with the vernacular of modern industry. Yu Xiuhua is a peasant with cerebral palsy who writes arresting love poems, the most famous of which is "Crossing Half of China to Sleep with You." Fan Yusu works as a nanny in Beijing and became a literary sensation after her autobiographical essay "I am Fan Yusu" went viral online in 2017. This group of women writers showcases the vibrant energy from a social stratum that had been often forgotten by the contemporary literary world.

Besides mainland China, the register "Chinese" oftentimes includes two other regions, Taiwan and Hong Kong, in the so-called "Greater China" area. Taiwan, a colony of the Japanese Empire between 1895 and 1945, further experienced harrowing pains during the "White Terror" era (1947–1987) under the rule of the Chinese Nationalist Party. The local history and politics are often narrated, alluded to, or allegorized in contemporary Taiwanese women writers' literary works. Li Ang's short stories collected in *The Butcher's Wife and Other Stories* and her first novel *The Lost Garden* are poignant and penetrating tales of gender and sexuality, ethnic identity and political persecution, and Taiwan's socio-economic landscape. Another prominent Taiwanese writer, Chu T'ien-wen (a.k.a. Zhu Tianwen), not only authored the widely acclaimed short story collection *Fin de siècle Splendor*, but has also produced numerous screenplays for director Hou Hsiao-hsien (from *A Time to Live, A Time to Die* to *Flowers of Shanghai* to the most recent *The Assassin*) since 1983. Chu T'ien-wen's younger sister Chu T'ien-hsin (a.k.a. Zhu Tianxin) is also an accomplished writer known for her intellectual and erudite fiction, such as *The Old Capital*, about the history of Taiwan after World War II.

Perhaps due to Taiwan's own obscure position in the contemporary world order, Taiwanese writers are more conscious of identity issues. Before any mainland Chinese writer was permitted to mention homosexuality in their literary works, Taiwanese women writer Chen Jo-hsi (a.k.a. Chen Ruoxi) wrote the novel *Paper Marriage* in 1986, later adapted into Ang Lee's award-winning film *Wedding Banquet*. The protagonist of Chu T'ien-wen's novel *Notes of a Desolate Man* is about a 40-year-old gay man, whose monologues embody the author's feminist prophecy for the postindustrial society. Chiu Miao-chin's (a.k.a. Qiu Miaojin) *Notes of a Crocodile*, a novel about queer teenagers in Taiwan in the form of a mixture of self-absorbed notes, diary entries, and allegories, appeared one year before the author's suicide. Through these writers' explorations of transgressive gender identities, readers can appreciate the robust queer politics in contemporary Taiwan that give the island a distinct cultural identity in Asia.

The history of Hong Kong was not as fraught as those of mainland China and Taiwan, but Hong Kong women writers possess distinct literary styles and addresses their own unique issues. The most celebrated woman writer in Hong Kong is Xi Xi. Her 1983 short story "A Woman Like Me" questions the arbitrary separation between the world of the living and the world of the dead. Her novel *My City* depicts the lives of ordinary Hong Kong citizens from a child's perspective; in whimsical language, she deconstructs the knowledge, hierarchy, anthropocentrism, and technocentrism of the modern world. Xi Xi's autobiographical novel *Mourning a Breast* contains the writer's philosophical reflections about gender, life, and established social concepts. Another prolific Hong Kong writer Lee Pik-Wah (a.k.a. Li Bihua) excels at transforming historical tales and legends into beautiful but tragic love stories. Some of Lee's novels have been adapted into classic films such as *Farewell My Concubine* and *The Green Snake*. Wong Pik-wan (a.k.a. Huang Biyun) is another unique voice in contemporary Hong Kong literature. She writes violent, sadistic, and even morbid stories, such as "Losing the City" and "She's a Young Woman and So Am I," depicting the loneliness, uncertainty, fear, and dark desires of Hong Kong residents.

Chinese women's writing should not be used as a kaleidoscope with which to peep into an exotic and immutable China; on the contrary, readers will encounter many different Chinas and evolving gender imaginations in those literary works. Ultimately it is the human stories, familiar or unfamiliar, dismal or joyful, sentimental or philosophical, that connect the East with the West.

# Hong Kong Writing

Andrea Lingenfelter

Don't listen to the naysayers – Hong Kong has long enjoyed a vibrant literary culture. Our focus here is fiction written in Chinese and translated into English, but this cosmopolitan metropolis also boasts a long list of writers who work in other languages, including English. Given Hong Kong's diversity, it's not at all surprising that contemporary Hong Kong fiction offers something for just about anyone, from cyber thrillers to martial arts epics, from Kafkaesque transformation stories and fractured fairy tales to historical fiction with a twist.

Looking back to the middle of the last century, the brilliant, Shanghai-born Eileen Chang (a.k.a. Zhang Ailing) spent time in this city during the war with Japan, and works like the title novella in the collection *Love in a Fallen City* (translated by Karen S. Kingsbury, 2006) and to a lesser extent *Lust, Caution* (translated by Julia Lovell, 2007) contain vivid descriptions of the city, its landscape, its cosmopolitanism, and the complex social relationships engendered by this mix. The Chinese Civil War and subsequent establishment of the People's Republic of China led to new influxes of immigrants to the then British Crown Colony, and Hong Kong became a space in-between, where writers uncomfortable with either Beijing or Taipei were able to read and write without official interference. In Hong Kong, the availability of the whole gamut of Sinophone literature, in addition to a huge variety of world literature, created fertile ground for the imaginations of local writers. This in turn fostered an eclecticism and cosmopolitanism which were nevertheless deeply rooted in Chinese literary style. Moreover, given Hong Kong's (undeserved) reputation as a cultural desert, writers there could follow their creative impulses, relatively free from scrutiny.

Post-war transplants to Hong Kong included popular writers like Xu Xu (1908–1980), who moved to Hong Kong in 1950 from Shanghai by way of Beijing and France. A collection of his fiction, *Bird Talk and Other Stories by Xu Xu: Modern Tales of a Chinese Romantic* (translated by Frederik Green) was published in May 2020. Xu Xu was a reluctant transplant to Hong Kong, and much of his post-war fiction is filled with nostalgia. As Xu Xu's translator Frederik Green observes, the theme of nostalgia 'At the same time it allowed him to explore a metaphysical homelessness …. bound up with the experience of modernity and that has driven many twentieth-century artists to reject a purely scientific depiction of reality and instead seek alternative realities within dreams or the fantastic.'[*] It is worth noting that Xu Xu also wrote light-hearted stories about his adopted home. Although banned in the mainland for decades, with left-

---

[*]   *Bird Talk and Other Stories, by Xu Xu: Modern Tales of a Chinese Romantic*, translated by Frederik Green (Stone Bridge Press, 2020), page 23.

wing critics in China labeling his works 'escapist,' which was code for politically unacceptable, his fiction is now quite popular there and has been the basis for many TV adaptations.

The most famous post-war Hong Kong literary figure has to be Jin Yong (a.k.a. Louis Cha Leung-yung, 1924 – 2018), the best-selling author of martial arts and knight errantry (*wuxia*) fiction. Born in Zhejiang province and educated in Chongqing and Suzhou, Jin Yong became a journalist and worked as a translator in Shanghai for a newspaper. He moved to Hong Kong in 1948 and stayed for the rest of his life. In 1959 he co-founded the newspaper *Ming Pao*, which published many of his novels in serial form. Jin Yong's novels have been translated into many languages, including English, and have also been adapted into films and television programs. He brought great literary flair to what had been a formulaic and lowbrow genre, earning him accolades among a diverse readership. An occasional critic of both the Nationalist and Communist governments, he had the distinction of being banned for periods of time in both mainland China and Taiwan. English translations of Jin Yong's novels include: *A Hero Born* (*Legends of the Condor Heroes* #1, translated by Anna Holmwood, 2018); *A Bond Undone* (*Legends of the Condor Heroes* #2, translated by Gigi Chang, 2020); *A Snake Lies Waiting* (*Legends of the Condor Heroes* #3, translated by Gigi Chang and Anna Holmwood, 2020); *A Heart Divided* (*Legends of the Condor Heroes* #4, translated by Gigi Chang and Shelly Bryant, 2021); *The Book and the Sword* (translated by Graham Earnshaw, 2019); *The Deer and the Cauldron* (three volumes, translated by John

Minford, 1997, 2000, and 2003); and *Fox Volant of the Snowy Mountain* (translated by Olivia Mok, 2020). Other works by Jin Yong have been adapted into English-language comic books and include the titles *The Heaven Sword and Dragon Saber* (by Ma Wing-shing), *The Legendary Couple* (by Tony Wong), and *The Return of the Condor Herœs* (by Wee Tian Beng).

In terms of literary fiction, Xi Xi (b. 1938) is the undisputed doyenne of literary and experimental fiction in Hong Kong. A documentary about her life and work played to sold-out houses in Hong Kong cinemas. Xi Xi has received international recognition for her long and brilliant literary career (which also includes poetry), and she was recently awarded both the Newman Prize (2019) as well as the Cikada Prize (2020). Xi Xi counts the Italian fabulist Italo Calvino and his novel *Invisible Cities* (1972) as an influence, and much of her work can be described as having parable-like qualities. Novels in translation include *Flying Carpet: A Tale of Fertillia* (translated by Diana Yue, 2000) and *My City: A Hongkong Story* (translated by Eva Hung, 1993). Collections of Xi Xi's short fiction have appeared in English as well. These include *A Girl Like Me and Other Stories* (enlarged edition, multiple translators, 1996) and *Marvels of a Floating City and Other Stories: An Authorized Collection* (edited by Eva Hung, translated by John Dent-Young and Esther Dent-Young, 1997). Xi Xi has also written a number of what could be described as 'fractured fairy tales,' some of which have been translated by Jennifer Feeley and which can be found online at sites like Words Without Borders. Dr. Feeley (who translated Xi Xi's delightfully witty poetry for the collection *Not Written Words*, 2016) is currently translating Xi Xi's genre-defying memoiristic postmodern novel, *Mourning a Breast*.

Carrying on this eclectic and fabulist tradition is a group of younger Hong Kong writers, including Dung Kai-cheung (b. 1967), Hon Lai Chu (b. 1978), and Dorothy Tse (b. 1977). Dung's *Atlas: The Archæology of an Imaginary City* (Weatherhead, 2012; translated by the author, along with Bonnie S. McDougall and Anders Hansson), like Xi Xi's *Marvels of a Floating City*, contains many echoes of Calvino and Borges. Leo Ou-fan Lee has suggested the same, adding that the book is 'a cross between fact and fiction, history and mystery... defies all generic categories and now stands as a contemporary classic.' Dung continues to chronicle Hong Kong's alternative history in *The History of the Adventures of Vivi and Vera* (Muse, 2018; translated by Yau Wai-ping). Set in the final decades of colonial rule, this novel, in the words of David Der-wei Wang, 'projects a futuristic vision in which postcolonial nostalgia meets postmodernist fantasia, and family romance begets science fantasy.' Dung ventures further into speculative fiction in his *Ghost in the Shell*-inspired 2018 novel *Beloved Wife*, a portion of which appears in *Chinese Literature Today* (v. 9, no. 1, 2020; translated by Andrea Lingenfelter). Dung's collection of short fiction, *Cantonese Love Stories: Twenty-five Vignettes* is also available in English (Penguin China, 2017; translated by Bonnie S. McDougall and Anders Hansson).

Under the auspices of the Hong Kong Atlas project, another 10 books of Sinophone Hong Kong writers in translation are being published. The project, which borrows its name from Dung Kai-cheung's novel, was launched around 2011 by a consortium of publishers, with funding from the Hong Kong Arts Development Council. Two collections of short fiction by two of Hong Kong's leading Surrealists, Hon Lai Chu and Dorothy Tse, have been published as part of this initiative. Hon Lai Chu's collection, *The Kite Family* (Muse, 2015; translated by Andrea Lingenfelter) also received funding from the National Endowment for the Humanities (US). Hon's writing is often compared to that of Franz Kafka. Her characters navigate a dangerous world fraught with absurdity. In one tale, a man transforms himself into a piece of furniture, pleasing the mother who accused him of being a slacker. In another tale, a collection of people find semi-permanent housing in a spartan hotel, after the sudden and unexplained implosion of their high-rise apartment building. Dorothy Tse, whose collection *Snow and Shadow* (Muse; translated by Nicky Harman) was published in 2014, also writes of social and familial dysfunction and is especially powerful in her exploration of the psychosexual fallout of poverty, patriarchy, and official negligence. Dorothy Tse's first novel *Owlish* has been translated by Natascha Bruce, and is due out with Fitzcarraldo (UK) and Grayworld (US) in 2023. Bruce describes it as 'on the one hand a cynical fairy tale about a middle-aged literature professor's love affair with the ballerina figure, and on the other a biting insight into the story of Hong Kong, both past and present.'

Readers who like an extra helping of context with their fiction might also want to check out a collection of short stories edited and translated by Monika Gaenesausber and Nicholas Olczak, *Of forests and humans: Hong Kong contemporary short fiction* (2020). This slim book contains stories by an eclectic group of authors (Sharon Chung, Xi Xi, Hon Lai Chu, Chan Lai Kuen, Wang Pu, and Jesse Chu), supplemented by thoughtful essays.

Recently we learned of yet another series devoted to Sinophone Hong Kong literature in translation, this time launched by the Chinese University of Hong Kong and Columbia University Press. This project will see a bundle of books published in 2021 that includes Liu Yichang's novel *The Drunkard* (translated by Charlotte Yiu), *Dragons: Shorter Fiction of Leung Ping Kwan* (translated by Wendy Chan, Jasmine Tong Man, and David Morgan), and *The Teddy Bear Chronicles*, by Xi Xi, (translated by Christina Sanderson). Described by the publisher as the first stream of conscious novel written in Chinese, *The Drunkard* (1962) chronicles its unnamed narrator's 'inexorable descent through the seedy bars and night-clubs of Hong Kong.' Perhaps best known as a poet, the author of *Dragons*, Leung Ping Kwan (also known as P K Leung and by the pen name Yesi / Ye Si) also turned his imagination to works of fiction, remarking that 'I have drawn on magical realism to explore the absurdity of Hong Kong.' *Dragons* promises to be a fascinating read. And, last but not least, *The Teddy Bear Chronicles* showcases Xi Xi's uniquely serious whimsy. Part picture book, part cultural history, this delightful work includes images of some of the teddy bears the author has made by hand and costumed as important figures from Chinese history. The full color images are accompanied by brief essays about these historical personages and their clothing. Delightful!

If you prefer mysteries, Chan Ho-kei (b. 1975) already has two novels out in English translation, *The Borrowed* (Black Cat, 2017) and *Second Sister* (Black Cat, 2020), both translated by Jeremy Tiang. *The Borrowed* is a novel composed of a series of linked stories about a police detective. Each of the chapters of the novel, which could individually stand on their own as short stories, is set at a different important juncture in Hong Kong's recent history. The novel begins in the present day and moves backwards in time, with the final chapter set in 1967. Some knowledge of recent Hong Kong history is helpful, but this puzzle of a novel is a rewarding read even for those unacquainted with the intricacies of Hong Kong's recent history. Reading Chan's book is like peeling an onion, with each chapter revealing new information that complicates our understanding of all that has come before. *Second Sister* is the story of a young woman who enlists the help of a mysterious hacker in her quest for answers – and revenge – after cyberbullying drives her younger sister to suicide. Chan's capacious novel offers a sympathetic portrayal of the lives of tech-savvy teenagers and lampoons start-up business culture, while at the same time probing questions of ethics and justice.

Our list of Hong Kong writers would not be complete without Lee Pik-wah (also known as Lilian Lee and Li Bihua), the author of dozens of novels and screenplays. Lee's most internationally famous novel is *Farewell My Concubine* (translated by Andrea Lingenfelter, 1993), which was adapted into a 1993 film of the same name, directed by Chen Kaige. Set in the world of Peking Opera and spanning over a half-century, Lee's novel contains details and back stories that didn't make it to the screen. Also translated into English, *The Last Princess of Manchuria* (original title *Yoshiko Kawashima*, translated by Andrea Lingenfelter, 1992) is a fictionalized biography of the Manchu noblewoman turned spy, which explores issues of gender and ethnicity. Lee herself has adapted a number of her novels into screenplays, and many of the films are available with English subtitles, including *Rouge*, *Green Snake*, and *The Reincarnation of Golden Lotus*.

Another popular novelist whose work is on its way to being available in English is Sharon Chung. Jeremy Tiang is currently translating Chung's *Regret*, a sprawling family melodrama. Set in late-80s and early-90s Hong Kong, it follows the intrigues and transgressions of an immensely wealthy Chinese family who live in a mansion on the Peak. Call it the seamy underbelly of *Crazy Rich Asians*!

As you can see, Hong Kong writers have a great deal to offer to readers of all tastes and interests, and there seems to be more to choose from all the time. Watch this space!

Emily Xueni Jin

In 2015, the English translation of Liu Cixin's epic science fiction novel *The Three Body Problem* (translated by Ken Liu, 2014) won Best Novel at The Hugo Awards, an award often dubbed as the 'Oscars of science fiction and fantasy.' Since then, contemporary Chinese science fiction has received an unprecedented level of attention. For many Anglophone readers, *The Three Body Problem* was not only their first introduction to contemporary Chinese science fiction, but their primary encounter with contemporary Chinese fiction. From readers to book dealers to academics, from Barack Obama to Mark Zuckerberg, everyone seemed to be captivated by the trilogy, and consequently turned their eyes to contemporary Chinese science fiction as a whole. Writers, scholars, translators and others within China as well as the international community now speculate with excitement and trepidation what might become of contemporary Chinese science fiction, a previously marginalized niche that has recently emerged as one of the hottest topics inside and outside China.

Despite the foundational presence of the Anglophone

literary tradition in the genre, science fiction is no longer the preserve of English-language writers, and translated literature has begun to occupy a significant role in the global literary scene. Contemporary Chinese science fiction writing is a hybrid of China's own science fiction tradition and a multitude of influences from translated science fiction introduced into China a century ago. Yet today's Chinese science fiction could be viewed as Chinese writers extrapolating on and responding to concerns about their immediate social, political and cultural reality via the genre of science fiction.

This has given rise to a particular subgenre of Chinese science fiction: science fiction realism, a label first brought to the table by writer Han Song to describe contemporary Chinese science fiction. It refers to a movement of using science fiction to depict twenty-first century Chinese reality, as well as the near future. Scholar Mingwei Song (宋明炜) uses the term 'new wave' to describe a similar concept, 'an avant-garde cultural spirit that encourages readers to think beyond the conventional ways of perceiving reality and to challenge the commonly accepted ideas about what constitutes the existence and self-identity of a person surrounded by technologies of self, society, and governance.[*]' Rapid developments in the everyday reality of Chinese society, in particular the technological explosion, has induced a strong sense of future anxiety. Such accelerated

[*]  *The Reincarnated Giant: An Anthology of Twenty-First-Century Chinese Science Fiction*, Edited by Mingwei Song and Theodore Huters (Columbia University Press, 2018). From the chapter "Does Science Fiction Dream of a Chinese New Wave?" By Mingwei Song, available online here: https://www.cupblog.org/2018/09/27/book-excerpt-the-reincarnated-giant-an-anthology-of-twenty-fist-century-chinese-science-fiction/

development is exacting such a toll on our cognitive mind that we find ourselves struggling to understand and keep up with our reality. Like boats navigating a frenetic, stormy sea, we seek desperately to be anchored. Yan Feng (严锋), one of the first Chinese literary scholars to turn his attention to science fiction, claims that the world is harder to recognize day by day, and reality is now stranger than science fiction. Chinese people are overwhelmed with anxiety about the future and are seeking a new kind of 'spirituality,' defined as a kind of cognitive and emotional anchor in the face of reality's oscillation. This 'spirituality,' Yan elaborates, is a way to grapple with reality and imagine what the impending future might look like. Science fiction, the only genre that speaks consistently in the tense of the future, offers alternative visions of how a future a few decades down the line might look, and thus emerges as a solution.

As a tool that engenders 'spirituality,' science fiction offers new conceptual frameworks and helps its readers to plant their feet on the ground; it is perfect. As the writer Chen Qiufan elegantly puts it, 'science fiction plays the role of placating, counterbalancing and eliminating our anxiety towards the future.' Hence, science fiction in China has gradually grown apart from the recurring motifs of golden age science fiction writing involving spaceships, aliens, unchartered mysterious lands and distant planets. Instead, science fiction realism has become a genre that keenly reflects upon the immediate concerns of reality, draws the future closer to the present, and consequently induces greater stability in the reader's mind. 'When mainstream realism more or less lost touch with reality and thus could not avoid being marginalized in the field of literary production[*],' science fiction takes over.

Turning briefly to history, the obsession of contemporary Chinese science fiction writers and readers with science fiction realism is not, in fact, an isolated case that emerged out of thin air. What appears to be an unfamiliar phenomenon echoes a familiar theme. If we scale out and examine modern Chinese literary history, we discover that science fiction realism laid down its roots seven decades ago, right after the establishment of the People's Republic of China in 1949. Chinese science fiction writers responded to the Chinese state's attempt to popularize science and technology by writing books that emulated Soviet literature in its values, form and content, and focused on representing socialist reality. They imagined a technology-laden future for socialist China. Specifically, writer Zheng Wenguang, recognized as 'the founding father of Chinese science fiction,' defined this seemingly self-contradictory subgenre through a myriad of articles and literary commentaries written between 1950 and 1990. Interestingly, 'science fiction realism' first emerged as a derogatory expression used by Western writers to describe Zheng's works. They criticized him for imposing realism onto science fiction, a genre that, at least in the Anglophone tradition, was intended to embody the otherworldly, outlandish imaginations of stargazers, instead of keeping its feet on the ground. Zheng, however, chose to counteract such contempt by appropriating the term 'science fiction realism,'

---

[*]   as above.

twisting it around, and using it to denote the essence of the works created by himself and his peers in post-1949 China. Zheng further explains his artistic purpose in an article written post-1980: 'I wish to dedicate my artistic pursuit to revolutionizing science fiction in China by creating something that is similar to science fiction yet doesn't exactly look like science fiction. I want to apply ways of writing science fiction to the portrayal of reality; science fiction usually focuses on imaginary worlds, but I want to write about the real world.'

A myriad of contemporary Chinese science fiction writers, each with different styles and approaches, are following in Zheng's footsteps by 'writing about the real world,' writing real-life concerns and emotions, through the lens of an imagined future or an alternative world. Liu Cixin, a representative of the so-called 'hard' science fiction, laden with detailed descriptions of science and technology, has written largely under the influence of the American golden age of science fiction of the 1960s and 1970s with space imagination at its center. By depicting the distant universe with great verisimilitude and using fundamental human concerns of war, ethics and death as the supporting pillars to his stories, Liu draws his readers into alternative worlds that, at their very heart, echo the physical and psychological concerns of everyday reality. Han Song, with his unique, elusive and imagery-rich voice, mines the legacy of surrealism and draws inspiration from writers like Lu Xun, who approach the depiction of reality through metaphors and veiled acerbic social commentaries. Both writers, though starkly different in style, can be viewed through the lens of science fiction realism.

Fast-forward to a younger generation of contemporary science fiction writers currently active in the domestic and global publishing scene, and we can begin to see how science fiction realism is developing in various directions. These writers, primarily born in the decade after 1980, are exploring representations of reality via their own cultural and disciplinary lens. Chen Qiufan, whose style strongly resembles Pynchon-esque experimental writing, draws his inspiration from both cutting-edge science and folk culture. His stories, often set in a near-future, technologized Chinese society, cut to the heart of the prolonged debate around human-technology relationships and foreground topics such as alienation and demystification. He straddles the delicate line between imagination and reality, turbulence and stability, the traditional and the revolutionary. Hao Jingfang, a physicist and an economist, infuses her stories with a fundamentally humanistic philosophy and literalizes allegories to scrutinize contemporary and immediately relevant social issues. Bao Shu turns to classical texts as well as Chinese history and embraces the tradition of alternative history, using the past as a mirror to reflect upon the present, and as a foundation to imagine the future. Chi Hui, who fills her works with topics such as environmentalism, boundary-crossing and gender discussions, brings to the table a strong female voice and a progressive perspective. Last but not least, it is worth mentioning A Que, one of the youngest writers of this generation as well as a recent favorite of the international book market. His stories discuss the intricacies of human relationships and touch the hearts of readers with their emotionally powerful narrative.

As a future-oriented China grapples with the anxiety, the uncertainty and the psychological effects of technological explosion, science fiction can bridge the gap between the present and what is to come with an imaginary yet immersive version of the future, intensified by verisimilitude. However, the current reality that Chinese science fiction is responding to is not, in fact, specifically and exclusively 'Chinese.' As more and more Chinese science fiction is translated into other languages, a reader new to Chinese literature might discover, with delight and surprise, their own realities and concerns mirrored by its science fiction. Therefore, it is indeed helpful to read Chinese science fiction as a literature about our common world, instead of grasping onto the chimera of a unified, stereotypical 'Chineseness.' When mainstream realist literature falls short of representing the realness of an ordinary person's life, and often restricts itself to a single voice to describe how reality should be, science fiction taps into the dimension of mental and affective realness by equipping its readers with a cognitive anchor, while offering plenty of versions of alternative realities. It simultaneously reduces and enables uncertainty. Both Yan Feng and Han Song maintain that reality is stranger than science fiction; turning this phrase around, we can also claim that *science fiction is truer than reality*.

Rachel Cheung

With its cheesy titles (cases in point: *The Legendary
Mechanic*, *The Beautiful Wife of the Whirlwind Marriage*
and *Mommy, Please Marry My CEO Daddy*) and tacky book
covers, China's online literature was once easy to dismiss
as a collection of trashy novels read only by a small subset
of the internet community. But in the past decade, thanks
to a surge in mobile internet users – there were more than
one billion in China in 2020 – online literature has seen
an explosive growth in readership. What was once a niche
genre of lowbrow tales has now been transformed into
mainstream fiction.

The platforms where internet fiction is published,
browsed and read, such as Hongxiu, Jjwxc, Qidian and
Tencent's China Literature, have grown and merged into
corporate behemoths, attracting writers from all walks of
life across the country. A report released in February 2020
by the Chinese Academy of Social Sciences recorded 455
million web literature readers and 17.6 million authors by
that year.

Popular online works have been snapped up by China's film industry and adapted for the silver screen, feeding the domestic market's ferocious appetite for entertainment. They include the Chinese period drama *Nirvana in Fire* (2015) – more on that later – and the modern romantic drama *Love O2O* (2016). Online literature is no longer regarded as lightweight fiction for teenagers and young adults, but as intellectual property with the potential to become movies, television series, manga, animations and video games.

To appreciate the novels themselves, however, one must first understand the publishing model and the environment in which the genre thrives, the ecosystem that is critical in shaping online fiction's format and content. Unlike traditional print fiction, where authors earn royalties for every book sold, online writers publish in instalments, much in the same way as Charles Dickens published *Great Expectations* in serial format in a weekly literary magazine, or as Hong Kong writer Jin Yong released his *wuxia* novels in daily newspaper columns. Readers top up their digital wallets on platforms and pay per chapter. This set-up means there is little quality control or formal editing process, nor is there much of a threshold for new authors to enter the online publishing world.

The market is also extremely competitive. A book has to stand out from hundreds of titles in order to draw a significant reader following on a website. The platforms tend to pit works against each other and rank them according to page visits, which, as a result, encourages clickbait and fan engagement. It is therefore normal for successful web novels to be unusually long, as the financial rewards are in proportion to their length. On the other hand, titles are frequently cancelled because of low readership.

In addition, the platforms manage readers' expectations by attaching hashtags to each title, labelling whether they have a good or a bad (= happy or unhappy) ending, whether the characters are strong, and whether the protagonists are loyal to each other.

In recent years, the industry has seen rapid expansion as well as major acquisitions online literature platforms by Chinese tech giants such as Alibaba and Tencent. During the coronavirus pandemic, online literature received a boost from a population trapped at home. Yet, as close observers believe, Chinese online literature has passed its heyday in terms of creativity and diversity.

As most authors are not professional writers or even particularly educated, web novels are not notable for their literary merits or polished style. Rather, they offer something even rarer: the Chinese Dream. This Chinese Dream is not the one defined by Xi Jinping, but one that belongs to the country's ordinary citizens, with grassroots voices that are usually drowned out by the government's narrative. This dream, however, is not in any way based in reality. Rather, these works are a form of escapism for both writers and readers. Yet, although the tales are far-fetched and sometimes bizarre, they do reveal the writers' and readers' suppressed desires and unrealised aspirations, as well as hinting at society's values and issues related to people's emotional satisfaction.

In online novels, writers paint alternative universes and create fictional worlds, where the characters exercise control over their own destinies, even if these fictitious realms are entirely devoid of logic. Online literature encompasses a wide range of themes: romance, fantasy, historical dramas, military narratives, gender-swapping stories, time and space travel. Central to the plot is often an all-powerful protagonist, who easily overcomes all obstacles, accumulates great wealth and defeats all enemies – ideally by humiliating their adversaries in the process.

Romance novels tend to be modern Cinderella tales with Chinese characteristics. The female archetype is a beautiful girl who discovers her aristocratic roots; she marries into an affluent family where her doting husband exacts revenge on all who have ever looked down on her. Equally telling are the characters whom the writers cast as villains in this type of story. One antagonist archetype is the 'white lotus' – female characters who appear innocent and demure, but are in fact manipulative and deceiving. Another is the 'green tea bitch' – female characters who are sexually promiscuous and steal other people's partners, but again, give the impression of being pure and gullible.

Fantasy novels often draw from elements of Japanese manga, and match characters with a specific theme, whether it is military (although the Chinese government now disapproves of military-themed novels and has banned many since 2019), farming, cooking or *xianxia*, a genre where the characters train to become immortals. Much like the regular plot lines in popular anime, protagonists battle new enemies in each story arc. They are, however, distinguished by their exceptional abilities to override the system and defeat institutions with unfailing luck.

The stories often expose issues that are prevalent in contemporary Chinese society, whether bribery, corruption or nepotism, yet instead of offering any meaningful critique, protagonists often overcome them by beating the culprit at their own game, having better connections or gaining more power.

In recent years, novels with original characters and plots have become harder to find, as authors increasingly conform to type and recycle tired tropes. As the industry matures, publishers invest resources in existing writers and works with greater commercial value, making it far more difficult for newcomers to gain a foothold. The heaviest blow, however, has come from the Chinese government's iron grip on the internet. Most online stories take place in fictional worlds where authors can avoid run-ins with politically sensitive issues — but online literature's growing influence has attracted increasing scrutiny from the authorities. With every change in government guidelines, chapters are redacted and titles suspended, some are even removed from the platforms completely. In serious cases, crackdowns on pornographic content have seen hefty prison sentences slapped on writers for disseminating obscene articles.

The directive issued in June 2020 by the State Administration of Press Publication, Radio, Film and Television (SAPPRFT) might be the harshest of them all – deciding not only what writers cannot write, but also what they can write. Authors are required to fall in line and register under their real names. Publishers are required to ensure that works 'correctly guide public opinion,' are 'healthy and positive,' and aligned with core socialist values; even the comments sections.

The following selection draws from novels published prior to the early 2010s, when the online publishing scene was at its most vibrant with ideas. The titles are among a small but growing number of works now translated into English by amateurs, as well as translations aided by artificial intelligence tools by platforms seeking overseas expansion.

First published online in 2006, *The Rankings of Lang Ya* by Hai Yan is a great option for readers making a first foray into Chinese online literature. It is better known by the title of its TV adaptation, *Nirvana in Fire*, staring actors Hu Ge, Wang Kai and Liu Tao, which became a roaring success in 2015. This historical novel tells the story of Lin Shu, a commander who was framed as a traitor and returned to the capital under a new alias to vindicate his family's name. While revenge plots featuring conniving palace concubines have become a cliché in Chinese period novels, *The Rankings of Lang Ya* stands out for its intricate plot, layered characters and poetic language, placing it in the ranks of classic *wuxia* novels.

With nearly 1,900 chapters published over three years on books.qq.com since 2017, *National School Prince Is A Girl* by Warring Young Seven is a typical web novel in terms of its length. Adapted into manga form and now also available in English on the platform WebNovel (Qidian's international branch) the story ticks many boxes in terms of elements commonly found in the genre. The story is interwoven with multiple themes: reincarnation, which gives the protagonist memories of a previous life, superhuman powers and a double identity, and gender-swapping, in which the female protagonist disguises herself as a teenage school boy. Set against the background of a modern Chinese city, the two main protagonists are professional gamers and corporate executives who are, at the same time, a hacker and a military leader engaged in a cat-and-mouse chase. The extensive description of gaming battles and strategies may not be for everyone, but it is reflective of the e-sports craze that has taken over China in recent years.

While publishing platforms are typically geared towards heterosexual readers, male or female, some platforms also reserve a section for queer literature, known in Chinese as 'dan mei' (耽美). This section consists of romanticised fantasies of male gay love written by female writers for female readers. Though this subgenre has a significant following online, it has been targeted by the authorities, whose attitude towards homosexuality remains conservative. In one of the most controversial cases, an author who wrote homoerotica under the pseudonym Tianyi was sentenced to over ten years in jail in 2018, on the charge of producing and selling pornographic materials for a book, titled *Occupy*.

However, despite the risk, authors continue to produce notable works under this subgenre.

Among them is Priest, a prolific writer who has consistently ranked among the most influential female authors in online literature, and has been critical in taking the 'dan mei' subgenre mainstream. Her spectacular world-building and evocative storytelling convinced Chinese entertainment companies to adapt her books for the big screen – albeit significantly toning down the romantic element and depicting the central relationships as being about brotherhood rather than homosexual attraction. Her works include *The Legend of Fei* (2020) and *Guardian* (2018). The latter is adapted from a gripping mystery novel of the same name, published on Jjwxc from 2012–2013. It follows a detective and a professor as they investigate supernatural phenomena, trace the origins of four holy artifacts and, in the process, discover their own identities, drawing readers into the fascinating world of Chinese mythology.

While China's clampdown on online literature has left questions about the future of the genre, one thing is without doubt: during the years when it was allowed to thrive, writers produced literary works that will likely outlast the platforms and the regime. With the creativity they have shown, these authors and their works might just be able to circumvent any restrictions imposed from above.

STOP PRESS: In December 2021, the novels of MXTX, another *danmei* writer, will appear in print in English translation for the first time. See https://sevenseasdanmei.com/

AUTHORS

# A YI
阿乙 (1976–)

A Yi was born Ai Guozhu in Ruichang, a city in Jiangxi Province, eastern China. His parents urged him to become a policeman but A Yi was passionate about writing. After failing the college entrance exam, however, he initially did become a policeman. Unhappy at his job, he worked at a local government agency and eventually, he became a sports editor at the *Zhengzhou Evening News* (郑州晚报).

A Yi began writing fiction at the age of 32, and credits his life experiences for his inspiration: his style tends towards brutalist existentialism, set within a crime or detective framework. Most of his short stories were initially published on his blog, and in 2008 he published a collection in print, entitled *Gray Stories* (灰故事, untranslated). His first novella was *A Perfect Crime* (下面，我该干些什么). His major novel *Wake Me Up at Nine in the Morning* (早上九点叫醒我, English forthcoming) was published in 2018.

In 2015, A Yi was invited to be the writer-in-residence at the OWSpace bookstore in Beijing.

## Selected Works

novels

*Zaoshang Jiudian Jiaoxing Wo* 早上九点叫醒我, 2018. Translated by Nicky Harman as *Wake me up at Nine in the Morning* (Oneworld Publications, forthcoming)

*Xiamian, wo gai gan xie shenme* 下面，我该干些什么 (2011). Translated by Anna Holmwood as *A Perfect Crime* (Oneworld Publications, 2015)

# AH CHENG
## 阿城 <sup>(1949–)</sup>

阿城 (1949–)

Zhong Acheng, more commonly known by his pseudonym Ah Cheng, is a contemporary novelist, scriptwriter, and painter most notable for pioneering the 'root-seeking' literary movement during the 1980s (known as *xungen wenxue* 寻根文学 in Chinese). Born in Beijing in 1949, his educational trajectory was cut short when he was sent to Shanxi and then Inner Mongolia as one of the Cultural Revolution's 'sent-down youth'. During his time in the countryside, Ah Cheng picked up painting, which would greatly inform his writing in the years to come.

After the Cultural Revolution, Ah Cheng returned to Beijing and started a career in literature and scriptwriting. In 1984 he published *King of Chess* (棋王). Later translated separately by both Bonnie McDougall and W.J.F. Jenner, it is a tale of transformation, resilience, and friendship, and has been hailed as 'one of the best novellas in post-Mao China.' In 1986, his novella trilogy – comprising *King of Children* (孩子王), *King of Chess*, and *King of Trees* (树王) – was published; each of the stories was subsequently adapted into a film. Ah Cheng also wrote the screenplays for *Hibiscus Town* (芙蓉镇, 1986), *Full*

*Moon in New York* (三个女人的故事, 1989), and *The Go Master* (吴清源, 2006).

In 1992, Ah Cheng received the Italian 'International Nonino Prize' for his literary achievements. In 1995, his travel journal, *Venetian Diary* (威尼斯日记, untranslated), won a major literary prize in Taiwan. More recently, he served as a scriptwriter for *The Assassin* (刺客聂隐娘), a martial arts blockbuster for which Hou Hsiao-hsien won the Best Director award at the 2015 Cannes Film Festival. In 2016, he published a collection of non-fiction and cultural criticism.

Ah Cheng is remarkable in his ability to reimagine the Cultural Revolution through the lens of Daoism and Confucianism, and he's considered one of the first Mainland Chinese writers to begin reconnecting China's literary language with its roots after the political strictures of the 50s, 60s and 70s. By deprioritising themes of violence and self-pity, he reintroduced a pluralistic, imaginative, and nuanced aspect of Chinese literature.

## Selected Works

novellas
*Shu Wang* 树王 (1986). Translated by Bonnie McDougall as *The King of Trees: Three Novellas* (New Directions Publishing, 2010)

ML

the
KING
of
TREES

AH CHENG

translated by
Bonnie S. McDougall

# ALAI
阿来 <sup>(1959–)</sup>

Yan Yongrui, more commonly known as Alai, is a writer, editor, and poet of Tibetan descent. Born in Barkam, a Tibetan autonomous prefecture in Sichuan, he wrote poetry before publishing his first novel, *Red Poppies* (尘埃落定), in 1998. The novel chronicles the rise and fall of a Tibetan family during an era of rapid modernization. It is told through the perspective of the son, who suffers from an intellectual disability. In 2000, Alai became the first author of Tibetan descent to win the Mao Dun Literature Prize. In 2005, he published *King Gesar* (格萨尔王) and *Hollow Mountain* (空山). In 2019, *Red Poppies* was named as one of the top seventy books of fiction that had shaped post-Mao China.

As an editor, Alai is known for his work at *Grassland* (草原) and *Science Fiction World* (科幻世界). During his tenure as editor-in-chief of *Science Fiction World*, the magazine became one of the largest-circulating science fiction magazines in the world. He was also the recipient of the Dangdai Literary Prize in 1989 and the Ethnic Minority Literature Award in 2009. In 2019, he became a member of the Standing

Committee of the Sichuan Provincial People's Congress. The same year, he wrote the screenplay for *The Climbers* (攀登者), a biopic on Chinese mountain climbers starring Zhang Ziyi.

Alai is most notable for reimagining, narrating, and illustrating Tibetan life through poetic imaginations and magic realism – in an age where representing Tibet is often both trying and challenging.

## Selected Works

novels

*Chen'ai Luoding* 尘埃落定 (1998). Translated by Howard Goldblatt and Sylvia Li-chun Lin as *Red Poppies* (Houghton Mifflin, 2002)

*Gesa'er Wang* 格萨尔王 (2009). Translated by Howard Goldblatt as *King Gesar* (Canongate Press, 2012)

*Tibetan Soul: Stories*, translated by Karen Gernant and Chen Zeping (MerwinAsia, 2012)

ML

# ANNI BAOBEI (ANNIE BABY)

安妮宝贝 <sup>(1974– )</sup>

Li Jie, more commonly known as Anni Baobei, is a contemporary novelist who has gained substantial popularity as an internet writer.

Born in Ningbo in 1974, she first published her writing on the literary website, *Under the Banyan Tree* (榕树下), while working at a bank. Uninspired by her job, she started unpacking themes of isolation, despair, and emotional intimacy through her online writings. In 2000, she published *Goodbye Vivian* (告别薇安 ), her first collection of short stories, centred around a female psyche. It has since sold over half a million copies, and was later adapted into the award-winning film *Soulmate* (七月与安生). In 2012, the stories 'Goodbye, An', 'Endless August', and 'The Road of Others' were translated and published in English under the title *The Road of Others*. Her other works, such as *Flowers of the Far Shore* (彼岸花), and *Lotus* ( 莲花) have not been translated, but have cult-like followings.

In 2016, Anni Baobei published a collection of short stories under a new pen name, Qing Shan (庆山). In 2019, she published her newest novel, *Xia Mo Shan Gu* (夏摩山谷, untranslated).

Anni Baobei is best known for her intimate portrayals of isolation, solitude, and urban materialism. As one of the earliest cyber writers to secure national commercial success, she unpacks the rugged realities of the one-child generation. To date, she has over 11 million followers on Chinese social media platform Weibo. She lives in Beijing and maintains a low profile.

## Selected Works

NOVELS

*The Road of Others*. Translated by Keiko Wang and Nicky Harman (Make-Do Publishing, 2012)

ML

# BAO SHU
宝树 (李峻) <sup>(1980– )</sup>

Bao Shu is the pen name of Li Jun (李峻), a science fiction and fantasy writer born in the eighties. He made his name as a writer when he released *Three Body X* (三体 X：观想之宙, published as *The Redemption of Time* in Ken Liu's translation), which is a sequel to Liu Cixin's (刘慈欣) 'The Remembrance of Earth's Past' (地球往事) series. Bao completed the 100,000-character fanfic follow-up in roughly three weeks after reading the last book in Liu's trilogy, *Death's End* (死神永生), on his computer—his friend scanned every page to send him while he was studying in Belgium for his second Masters degree. In 2011, Liu Cixin authorised the publication of the sequel, putting Bao on track to become a full-time writer. Bao's stories combine elements of classical Eastern and Western philosophy and Chinese history with his imaginings of alternative histories and possible futures. They have earned him six Nebula Awards for Science Fiction and Fantasy in Chinese, three Galaxy Awards for Chinese Science Fiction, and a nomination for the Grand Media Award for Chinese Literature.

## Selected Works

NOVELS

*Santi X: guanxiang zhi miao* 三体X：观想之宙 (Chongqing Publishing House, 2011). Translated by Ken Liu as *The Redemption of Time* (Head of Zeus, 2019)

short stories and novellas

*Liuxia Ta de Jiyi* 留下她的记忆 (*Super Nice Magazine*, 2012). Translated by Ken Liu as 'Preserve Her Memory' (*Clarkesworld*, issue 108, 2015)

*Da Shidai* 大时代 (mitbbs.com, 2012). Translated by Ken Liu as 'What Has Passed Shall in Kinder Light Appear' (*Fantasy and Science Fiction*, March/April 2015)

*Dengta shaonü* 灯塔少女 (Zui Mook, 2017). Translated by Andy Dudak as 'The Lighthouse Girl' (*Clarkesworld*, issue 136, 2018)

*Gulao de diqiu zhi ge* 古老的地球之歌 (New Star Press, 2012). Translated by Adrian Thieret as 'Songs of Ancient Earth', in *The Reincarnated Giant* (Columbia University Press, 2018)

*Renren dou ai cha'ersi* 人人都爱查尔斯 (*Science Fiction World*, 2014). Translated by Ken Liu as 'Everybody Loves Charles' (*Clarkesworld*, issue 112, 2016)

TH

# BI FEIYU

毕飞宇 (1964– )

Bi Feiyu is a professor of literature at Nanjing University, in Jiangsu province; he was born in the nearby city of Xinghua. He is the recipient of the Lu Xun Literary Prize and the Mao Dun Prize, two of China's highest national literary awards. Internationally, his novels have been longlisted for the Independent Foreign Fiction Prize, and in 2010 his novel *Three Sisters* (comprising three Chinese stories: 玉米, 玉秀, 玉秧) won the Man Asian Literary Prize. The novel explores the lives of three women during the Cultural Revolution. Through these individual lives, Bi Feiyu brought to life the society they lived in. In 2017 he was made a Chevalier de l'Ordre des Arts et des Lettres, one of France's highest honours, in recognition of his contribution to literature.

## Selected Works

NOVELS

*Tuina* 推拿 (2008). Translated by Howard Goldblatt and Sylvia Li-chun Lin as *Massage* (Penguin Random House Australia, 2015)

*Qing Yi* 青衣 (1999). Translated by Howard Goldblatt and Sylvia Li-chun Lin as *The Moon Opera* (Telegram Books, 2007)

*Yu Mi, Yu Xiu, Yu Yang* 玉米, 玉秀, 玉秧 (2003). Translated by Howard Goldblatt and Sylvia Li-chun Lin as *Three Sisters*, (Houghton Mifflin Harcourt, 2010)

ESSAYS

*Xiaoshuo Ke* 小说课 (2018). Translated by Nicky Harman as *Literary Lectures* [working title] (Routledge, forthcoming, 2022)

# CAO WENXUAN

曹文軒<sup>(1954–)</sup>

Cao Wenxuan is one of China's most popular authors of children's fiction. Now a professor of Chinese at Peking University and the Vice President of the Beijing Writers Association. The son of an itinerant principal of rural primary schools, he has used his childhood as inspiration for his writings, many of which are set in 1950s and 1960s rural China.

The *New York Times* noted: 'Sunshine and playtime are not the hallmarks of Cao Wenxuan's stories for children. Instead, there are mass starvation and displacement, flooding, plagues of locusts, and mental and physical disabilities. Yet Cao, 62, is among the most beloved writers in China.' (May 1, 2016)

He is praised for his meaningful stories and lyrical prose. As one Weibo commentator noted, 'His works were what our generation grew up reading, they were the books that accompanied us as we grew up.'

Cao has won most of the domestic prizes available to children's authors. *The Grass House* (草房子) and *Bronze and*

*Sunflower* (青铜葵花) are two of his books that have sold millions of copies and received awards, while his acclaimed *Dingding Dangdang* series follows the lives of two brothers with Downs Syndrome living in a small rural Chinese village.

In 2016, he became the first Chinese author to receive the Hans Christian Andersen Award, regarded as the foremost international honour for children's literature.

## Selected Works

NOVELS

*Qingting Yan* 蜻蜓眼 (2016). Translated by Helen Wang as *Dragonfly Eyes* (Walker, 2021)

*Qingtong Kuihua* 青铜葵花 (2005). Translated by Helen Wang as *Bronze and Sunflower* (Walker, 2015)

*Huang Liuli* 黄琉璃 (2008). Translated by Nicholas Richards as *The Amber Tiles* (Better Books, 2015)

*Cao Fangzi* 草房子 (1997). Translated by Julian Chen, Christopher Malone and Sylvia Yu as *The Grass House* (Long River Press, 2005)

PICTURE BOOKS

*Yumao*, 羽毛. Translated by Chlœ Garcia Roberts as *Feather* (Elsewhere, 2017)

SHORT STORIES

*Yige Jiao Feng de Gezi* 一只叫凤的鸽子. Translated by Helen Wang as 'A Very Special Pigeon'

ESSAYS

*Wuya* 乌鸦. Translated by Helen Wang as 'Crows' (Read Paper Republic, 2015)

FB

# CAN XUE
残雪 [(1953– )]

Deng Xiaohua, more commonly known as Can Xue, is an avant-garde fiction writer and literary critic. Widely regarded as one of the most experimental writers of her generation, her penchant for surrealism has fascinated global readers. Can Xue's pseudonym stands for 'residual snow,' which can simultaneously describe 'dirty snow that refuses to melt' and 'the purest snow at the top of a high mountain.'

Can Xue was born in Changsha, Hunan Province in 1953. Her father was the one-time editor-in-chief of the *New Hunan Daily* and was sent to a re-education camp in the late 1950s after being labelled an 'Ultra-Rightist.' Subsequently, her family relocated to the countryside.

Despite these difficulties, she educated herself and independently studied Western classics. She spent twenty years as a metalworker and a tailor before pursuing writing full-time. In 1985, she published her first novel, *Yellow-mud Street* (黄泥街, 1985). Can Xue's most notable works include *Five Spice Street* (五香街, 2009), *Frontier* (边疆, 2016), and *Love in the New Millennium* (新世纪爱情故事, 2018). In 2015,

*The Last Lover* (最后的情人, 2014) won the Best Translated Book Award from the University of Rochester. Her works of fiction are often grotesque but provide subversive glimpses of how the Cultural Revolution informed and disrupted human relationships.

Heavily influenced by Jorge Luis Borges, Dante Alighieri, and Franz Kafka, Can Xue's unconventional narratives are commonly described as both captivating and perplexing. In response to these assessments, she has stated: 'If a reader feels that this book is unreadable, then it's quite clear that they're not one of my readers.'

Most recently, she was nominated for the 2019 Nobel Prize in Literature. The same year, *Love in the New Millennium* was longlisted for the International Booker Prize.

## Selected Works

NOVELS

*Tuwei Biaoyan* 突围表演 (1988), later published as 五香街 (2002). Translated by Karen Gernant and Chen Zeping as *Five Spice Street* (Yale University Press, 2009)

*Zuihou de Qingren* 最后的情人 (2005). Translated by Annelise Finegan Wasmœn as *The Last Lover* (Yale University Press, 2014)

*Bianjiang* 边疆 (2008). Translated by Annelise Finegan Wasmœn as *Frontier* (Yale University Press, 2017)

*Xin Shiji Aiqing Gushi* 新世纪爱情故事 (2013). Translated by Annelise Finegan Wasmœn as *Love in the New Millennium* (Yale University Press, 2018)

SHORT STORY COLLECTIONS

*Tiantang li de Duihua* 天堂里的对话 (1988). Translated by Ronald
R. Janssen and Jian Zhang as *Dialogues in Paradise*, (Northwestern
University Press, 1989)

*The Embroidered Shoes*. Compiled and translated by Ronald R. Janssen
and Jian Zhang (Henry Holt & Co., 1997)

*Blue Light in the Sky and Other Stories*. Compiled and translated by
Karen Gernant and Chen Zeping (New Directions Publishing, 2006)

*Vertical Motion*. Compiled and translated by Karen Gernant and Chen
Zeping (Open Letter Press, 2011)

NOVELLAS

*Canglao de Fuyun*苍老的浮云 (1986) and *Huangni Jie* 黄泥街 (1987).
Compiled and translated by Ronald R. Janssen and Jian Zhang as *Old
Floating Cloud: Two Novellas* (Northwestern University Press, 1991)

ML

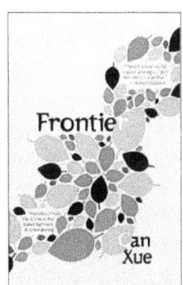

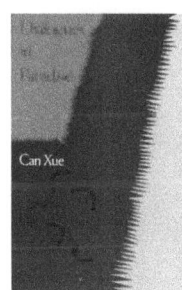

# CHAN HO-KEI

陳浩基 [(1975-)]

Chan Ho-Kei is a prolific mystery writer who was born and raised in Hong Kong. He has worked as a software engineer, scriptwriter, game designer and editor of comic magazines. His writing career started in 2008 at the age of 33, and his short story 'The Case of Jack and the Beanstalk' (傑克魔豆殺人事件, untranslated) was shortlisted for the Mystery Writers of Taiwan Award. He went on to win the award again the following year with 'The Locked Room of Bluebeard' (藍鬍子的密室, untranslated). In 2011, Chan's breakout novel, *The Man Who Sold the World* (遺忘・刑警, untranslated) won the prestigious Soji Shimada Mystery Award. He has since gone on to publish many popular mystery and thriller novels, and credits human curiosity as the driving force behind the genre.

## Selected Works

NOVELS:

*S.T.E.P.* (co-authored with Mr Pets/Wang Chien-Min). Translated by Jeremy Tiang as *The Borrowed* (Black Cat, 2017)

*Wangnei Ren* 網內人. Translated by Jeremy Tiang as *Second Sister*

(Grove Press, 2020)

SHORT STORIES:

*Ling Jian* 靈視. Translated by Kristen Robinson as 'Seeing Ghosts'
(Leeds Centre for New Chinese Writing, 2020)

AG

# CH'EN JO-HSI

陳若曦 (1938– )

Ch'en Jo-hsi (Chen Ruoxi) was born in Taiwan. She attended National Taiwan University, where she founded the journal *Modern Literature* (Xiandai Wenxue 现代文学) together with writer friends. She began writing while studying literature in the late 1950s. After graduation, she left for the United States to study English literature. In 1966, she and her husband moved to Beijing and then to Nanjing. The family lived in mainland China for seven years during the Cultural Revolution, until 1973, when they moved to Hong Kong. They later emigrated to Canada, and finally settled in the United States in 1979. Chen returned to Taipei in 1994.

Ch'en Jo-hsi is a novelist, essayist, and short-story writer, and also writes critical commentaries in the fields of politics, society, and literature. Her debut novel *The Weekend* (周末, untranslated) was published in Taiwan's *Literature Magazine* (文学杂志) when she was only nineteen years old.

Ch'en's best-known collection of short stories, *The Execution of Mayor Yin* (尹县长, 1978) was published in 1978, after the Cultural Revolution. The stories captured Ch'en's experiences during the Cultural Revolution; the collection is seen as being one of the seminal works of 'scar literature'.

In the 1980s, Ch'en became interested in the situation of Chinese women, and particularly that of Chinese female writers around the world. She became the president of the Overseas Chinese Women Writers' Association, and in 1988 she published a collection of short stories titled *A Daughter's House* (女儿的家, untranslated), which emphasized the urgent need for women to be self-reliant.

## Selected Works

SHORT STORY COLLECTIONS
*Yin Xian Zhang* 尹县长 (1978). Translated by Nancy Ing and Howard Goldblatt as *The Execution of Mayor Yin and Other Stories from the Great Proletarian Cultural Revolution* (Indiana University Press, 1978)
*The Old Man and Other Stories* (1986). Translated by Diane Cornell and others (Research Centre for Translation, Chinese University of Hong Kong, 1986)

ORIGINALLY IN ENGLISH
*Democracy Wall and the Unofficial Journals* (Institute of East Asian Studies, 1982)
*Ethics and Rhetoric of the Chinese Cultural Revolution* (1981). By Lowell Dittmer and Ch'en Jo-hsi (Institute of East Asian Studies, 1981)

TH

# CHEN QIUFAN
陈楸帆 [(1981–)]

Born in Guangdong, Chen Qiufan (aka Stanley Chan) is a science fiction writer, columnist, and scriptwriter. He graduated from Peking University with double honours in Chinese and Film, then studied Integrated Marketing Communications on a combined Hong Kong University / Tsinghua University programme, before working first for Baidu and now for Google.

Chen Qiufan has published over thirty stories in *Science Fiction World*, *Esquire*, *Chutzpah!* and other magazines, as well as a novella, *The Abyss of Vision* (2006), and novel *The Waste Tide* (荒潮, 2013). Chen is the winner of three Galaxy Awards for Chinese Science Fiction and twelve Nebula Awards for Science Fiction and Fantasy in Chinese. *The Fish of Lijiang* (丽江的鱼儿们), translated by Ken Liu, received the Best Short Form Award of the 2012 Science Fiction and Fantasy Translation Awards. English translations of his fiction have also been published in *Clarkesworld*, *Interzone*, and *Fantasy & Science Fiction*.

The Oxford Handbook of Modern Chinese Literature

notes that his first novel, *The Waste Tide*, 'combines realism with allegory to present the hybridity of humans and machines.' His fiction often revolves around issues of perception, and he has become known for his use of AI generated content in his writing. In 2020 his *State of Trance* (出神状态), included in the short story collection *The Book of Shanghai*, used AI-generated paragraphs based on his own writing and won an award, beating Nobel Laureate Mo Yan. He currently resides in Beijing.

## Selected Works

NOVELS

*Huang Chao* 荒潮 (2013). Translated by Ken Liu as *The Waste Tide* (Head of Zeus, 2019)

SHORT STORIES

*Chushen Zhuangtai* 出神状态. Translated by Josh Stenberg as 'State of Trance' in *The Book of Shanghai: A City in Short Fiction* (Comma Press, 2020)

*Lijiang de Yu'ermen* 丽江的鱼儿们 (2006). Translated by Ken Liu as 'The Fish of Lijiang' in *Invisible Planets* (Tor, 2016)

*Shu Nian* 鼠年 (2009). Translated by Ken Liu as 'The Year of the Rat' in *Invisible Planets* (Tor, 2016)

*Shazui zhi Hua* 沙嘴之花 (2012). Translated by Ken Liu as 'The Flower of Shazui' in *Invisible Planets* (Tor, 2016)

*Mai* 霾 (2010). Translated by Ken Liu and Carmen Liying Yan as 'The Smog Society'

*Mao de Linghun* 猫的灵魂 (2012). Translated by Ken Liu as 'The Mao Ghost'

*Kaiguang* 开光 (2012). Translated by Ken Liu as 'Coming of the Light'

*Silie de Yi Dai* 撕裂的一代 (2016). Translated by Ken Liu as 'The Torn Generation: Chinese Science Fiction in a Culture in Transition' (https://www.tor.com/2014/05/15/the-torn-generation-chinese-science-fiction-in-a-culture-in-transition/).

FB

# CHEN RAN
陈染 (1962– )

Chen Ran was born in Beijing. Her work is known
for exploring themes of female desire and psychological
detachment from society. To date, Chen has only published
one full length novel, her 1996 work *A Private Life* (私
人生活). However, she has published a number of short
story collections, including *The Words of Men, the Words of
Things, the Words of Dogs* (人語・物語・狗語, untranslated).
She has won a number of literary prizes, including the first
contemporary China Female Writer's Award.

Chen Ran's fiction explores the female psyche, often
reflecting on the loneliness and frustrations of youth, and *A
Private Life* is no exception. The novel relates the story of Ni
Niuniu from childhood to her thirtieth year. This coming
of age plotline encompasses Ni's psychological breakdown
and subsequent institutionalisation, along with her life of
seclusion following her release from a psychiatric hospital.
The action of the story takes place in Beijing against the
backdrop of the Cultural Revolution and the Tiananmen
Square protests in the spring and summer of 1989.

## Selected Work

NOVELS

*Siren Shenghuo* 私人生活 (2001). Translated by John Howard-Gibbon as *A Private Life* (Columbia University Press, 2004)

TH

# CHEN XIWO
陈希我 (born 1960s)

Chen Xiwo was born and brought up in Fujian, where he still lives. He teaches comparative literature at Fuzhou Normal University and has published seven novels and numerous novellas and short stories. He has long been an outspoken critic of Chinese government and society and it was nearly 20 years before his books could be published in China. In 2010, Asia Sentinel described Chen Xiwo as 'one of China's most outspoken voices on freedom of expression for writers'. One recurring theme in Chen's fiction is the relationship between sexual and social corruption, and perhaps his most famous work, the novella *I Love My Mum* (遮蔽) explores incest and S&M as metaphors for a dysfunctional society. His stories are often narrated by, and focus on, women and children, and are empathetic despite his uncomprising subject matter. His works have been nominated for several prizes and in 2001 he won the Chinese Literature Media Prize, with *Dissipation* (我们的苟且).

Chen Xiwo's short fiction, in particular, has aroused considerable interest among English-speaking readers, with his stories (complete or in excerpt) appearing in *Asymptote*, *Index on Censorship*, *Words without Borders* and the *Los Angeles Review of Books China Channel*.

SHORT STORY COLLECTIONS

*Maofan Shu* 冒犯书. Translated by Nicky Harman as *The Book of Sins* (MakeDo Publishing, 2014)

SHORT STORIES AND EXCERPTS

*Chong* 宠. Translated by Nicky Harman as 'Pet' (*Asymptote*, 2019)

*Pain* 我疼. Translated by Nicky Harman as 'Pain' (*Los Angeles Review of Books China Channel*, 2018)

*Dai Dao de Nan Ren* 带刀的男人. Translated by Nicky Harman as 'The Man with the Knife' (*Words Without Borders*, 2012)

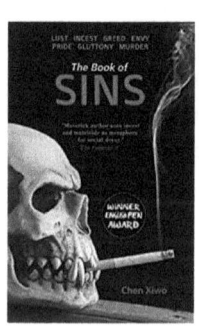

# CHI HUI
迟卉 (1984– )

Chi Hui was born in Jilin Province, in north-eastern China. From 2006 to 2010, she was the editor of, and a writer for, *Science Fiction World*, China's premiere genre magazine and the world's largest science fiction periodical in circulation. As an author, she has published under various pen-names: soulaxia, Snow Dance (雪舞风华), Black Kitten (黑小猫), Only Son (独子), Road of No Return (归者无路), and Bug's Nest (虫巢). She has garnered numerous nominations and honors, including a 2015 Chinese Nebula Silver Award (全球华语科幻星云奖) for her novel *Artificial Humanity 2075: Recombined Consciousness* (伪人2075·意识重组, untranslated).

## Selected Works

SHORT STORIES

*Yulin* 雨林. Translated by Lie Li as 'The Rain Forest', collected in *The Reincarnated Giant: An Anthology of Twenty-First-Century Chinese Science Fiction* (Columbia University Press, 2018)

*Weiren Suanfa* 伪人算法. Translated by John Chu as 'The Calculations of Artificials' in *Clarksworld* 121 (October 2016) and collected in *The Apex Book of World SF: Volume 5* (Apex Book Company, 2018)

*Shenhai Yu* 深海鱼. Translated by Brian Bies as 'Deep Sea Fish', collected in *The Magazine of Fantasy & Science Fiction*, March-April 2018 (Spilogale, 2018)

*Leng* 冷. Translated as 'The Cold' in *Ticket to Tomorrow and Other Stories* (The Commercial Press, 2019)

*Feixiang* 飞翔. Translated as 'Fly' in *Ticket to Tomorrow and Other Stories* (The Commercial Press, 2019)

*Huoyan Fengbao* 火焰风暴. Translated as 'Flame Storm' in *Ticket to Tomorrow and Other Stories* (The Commercial Press, 2019)

*Yu Chuan* 雨船. Translated by Andy Dudak as 'Rain Ship' in *Clarksworld* 125 (February 2017)

*Xin Lu* 星路. Translated as 'The Heaven-Moving Way' in *Apex Magazine* 125 (January 2018)

# CHI LI
池莉 (1957– )

Chi Li is a contemporary writer best known for bringing neorealism to Chinese literature. Born in Xiantao in Hubei Province, Chi Li now lives in the city of Wuhan. Prior to pursuing writing full-time, she studied and practiced medicine for the Wuhan Iron and Steel Corporation. During her time there, she spent an extensive amount of time with manufacturing workers and started writing about blue-collar livelihoods. In 1983, she enrolled in Wuhan University to study Chinese literature. In 1987, Chi Li published her first story, 'Frustrating Life' (烦恼人生 , 1987) in the literary magazine *Fragrant Grass* (芳草). The story chronicles the mundane life of a middle-aged factory worker and the day-to-day frustrations he encounters. The story became an instant success, and went on to win the prestigious Lu Xun Literary Prize. She later published an anthology of the same name. Throughout her career, Chi Li has produced critical works of neorealism, with narratives that are grounded, structurally simplistic, but painstakingly relatable. One of her most famous works, *Life Show* (生活秀, 2000), was later adapted into a television show and an award-winning film.

Influenced by the female psyche, ordinary lifestyles, and everyday dilemmas, Chi Li's writings are rhetorically visceral, culturally relevant, and emotionally layered – which is why many of her books are well-received and have been adapted into different media.

In addition to writing, Chi Li has also served as a delegate at the China's National People's Congress. Chi Li is a member of the China Writers Association, and currently serves as the president of the Wuhan Federation of Literary and Art Circles.

## Selected Works

**SHORT STORIES**

*Shenghuo Xiu* 生活秀 (2000). Collected in *The Life Show and Other Stories*, (Long River Press, 2012). Also translated by Karen Gernant and Chen Zepin as 'Life Show' (Iowa Writer's Program, 2014)

*Xi Yao* 细腰. Translated by Scott W. Galer as 'Willow Waist', collected in *Chairman Mao Would Not Be Amused: Fiction from Today's China* (Grove Press, 1995)

*Apart from Love*, collected short stories (Foreign Language Press, 1994). Translator[s] unnamed.

'Hot or Cold–Life's Okay' Translated by Michæl Cody, collected in Shu-ning Sciban and Fred Edwards, eds., *Dragonflies: Fiction by Chinese Women in the Twentieth Century* (Ithaca: East Asia Program, Cornell University, 2003)

ML

# CHI ZIJIAN
迟子建 (1964- )

Chi Zijian was born on the Sino-Russian border, in Mohe village in Heilongjiang Province. She graduated from Beijing Normal University and Lu Xun Writers Academy. She was also a 2005 resident of the International Writing Program at the University of Iowa in the United States. Her novel *The Last Quarter of the Moon* (额尔古纳河右岸) won the 2008 Mao Dun Prize for Literature. The novel tells the story of a nomadic reindeer-herding clan of the Evenki tribe in Northeastern China through the lens of an old woman. It is a sweeping epic about an extraordinary woman bearing witness to the stories of her tribe as well as the transformations in China during the twentieth century.

A prolific author with more than fifty short stories, novellas and novels under her belt, she has received all of China's major literary awards. While many of her contemporaries focus on urban life, she writes about rural people and stays close to the region of her birthplace. Six of her short stories have been translated and are collected in *Figments of the Supernatural*.

## Selected Works

NOVELS

*E-er-gu-na He You'an* 额尔古纳河右岸. Translated by Bruce Humes as *The Last Quarter of the Moon* (Vintage Books, 2014)

*Wan'an, Meigui* 晚安, 玫瑰. Translated by Poppy Toland as *Goodnight, Rose* (Viking China, 2019)

SHORT STORY COLLECTIONS

*Figments of the Supernatural*. Translated by Simon Patton (James Joyce Press, 2004)

BBS

# CHIU MIAO-CHIN

邱妙津 (1969-1995)

Chiu Miao-Chin (Qiu Miaojin) was a Taiwanese novelist. In 1991, she graduated from National Taiwan University with an undergraduate degree in Psychology. She then worked as a counselor and later as a reporter for the weekly magazine *The Journalist*. She moved to Paris in 1992, where she later pursued graduate studies in clinical psychology and feminism at the University of Paris VIII. Her first published story, 'Prisoner', received Taiwan's Central Daily News Short Story Prize, and her novella *Lonely Crowds* won the United Literature Association Award. While in Paris, she directed a thirty-minute film called *Ghost Carnival*. Soon afterwards, at the age of twenty-six, she committed suicide.

The posthumous publications of her novels *Last Words from Montmartre* (蒙马特遗书) and *Notes of a Crocodile* (鳄鱼手记) made her into one of the most revered countercultural icons in the Sinophone world. After her death in 1995, she was awarded Taiwan's *China Times* Honorary Prize for Literature. In 2007, a two-volume edition of her *Diaries* was published. In 2017, she became the subject of a feature-length documentary by Evans Chan, titled *Death in*

*Montmartre*. Qiu's films can be found in the collection of the Museum of Modern Art, New York. Her writing has had a profound influence on LGBT literature in Taiwan. Luo Yijun's book *Forgetting Sorrow* (遺悲懷, untranslated) was written in her memory.

## Selected Works

### NOVELS

*E'yu Shouji* 鳄鱼手记 (1994). Translated by Bonnie Huie as *Notes of a Crocodile* (New York Review of Books Classics, 2017)

*Mengmate Yishu* 蒙马特遗书 (1996). Translated by Ari Larissa Heinrich as *Last Words from Montmartre* (New York Review of Books Classics, 2014). Excerpt translated by Howard Goldblatt as *Letters from Montmartre*, in J. Lau and H. Goldblatt (eds) *The Columbia Anthology of Modern Chinese Literature* (Columbia University Press, 2007)

### SHORT STORIES

*Bolatu zhi Fa* 柏拉图之发. Translated by Fran Martin as *Platonic Hair*, collected in *Angelwings: Contemporary Queer Fiction from Taiwan* (University of Hawai'i Press, 1990)

BBS

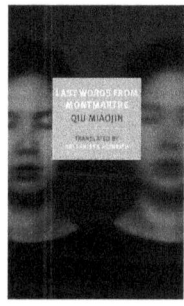

# CHU T'IEN-HSIN
朱天心 (1958- )

Chu T'ien-hsin comes from a family of Taiwanese writers. Her father Chu Hsi-ning (主西宁) was a writer of military-themed works, her mother Liu Mu-sha (刘慕沙) was a Japanese-Mandarin translator, and her older sister, Chu T'ien-wen (朱天文, see below), was the first woman to win the Newman Prize for Chinese Literature from the University of Oklahoma. Originally from Kaohsiung, Chu T'ien-hsin is considered Taiwan's authority on life among KMT military dependents' villages. She is a member of the Alliance of Ethnic Equality, a Taiwanese organization which opposes the exploitation of ethnic differences for political gain. Her 1984 novel, *The Last Train to Tamshui* (淡水最后列车), was adapted into a film by Ko I-chen.

## Selected Works

NOVELS AND NOVELLAS

*Gudu* 古都 (INK Publishing, 1997). Translated by Howard Goldblatt as *The Old Capital* (Columbia University Press, 2007)

*Danshui Zuihou Lieche* 淡水最后列车 (in *Wo Jide* 我记得, UNITAS Publishing, 2001). Translated by Michelle Yeh as *The Last Train to*

*Tamshui* (The Chinese Pen, 1988)

SHORT STORIES

*Xiang Wo Juancun de Xiongdimen* 想我眷村的兄弟们 (INK Publishing, 2002). Translated by Michelle Wu as *Epilogue: In Remembrance of My Buddies from the Military Compound* (In *The Last of the Whampoa Breed: Stories of the Chinese Diaspora*, Columbia University Press, 2003)

REC

# CHU T'IEN-WEN
朱天文 <sup>(1956– )</sup>

Chu T'ien-wen was born in Taipei into a literary family and is known for her short stories and screenplays. Both her sisters Chu T'ien-yi (朱天衣) and Chu T'ien-hsin (朱天心, see above) are writers. Chu T'ien-wen is well known for her multi-decade collaboration with the Taiwanese director Hou Hsiao-hsien (侯孝賢). Chu either wrote or co-wrote the screenplays for a number of Hou's most famous works, including *Cafe Lumiere* (咖啡时光), the *Millennium Mambo* (千禧曼波) and all the films in the 'Taiwanese History Trilogy.'

Alongside screenplays, Chu has also published a number of novels and short story collections. Her two most famous works are the short story collection *Fin de Siècle Splendour* (世紀末的華麗) and the novel *Notes of a Desolate Man* (荒人手記), published in 1990 and 1994 respectively, following the end of martial law in Taiwan in 1987. The title story in *Fin de Siècle Splendour* tells the story of a young woman named Mia, charting her development from a materialistic fashionista to a lover of nature – a journey Chu uses to comment on the tension between consumerism and the natural world. *Notes* tells the life stories of two Taiwanese gay men, Ah Yao and

Xiao Shao, and how their lives are disrupted by AIDS. Chu's short stories also received special mention in 2015, when she was awarded the Newman Prize for Chinese Literature.

## Selected Works

### NOVELS

*Huangren Shouji* 荒人手記 (1994). Translated by Howard Goldblatt and Sylvia Li-chun Lin as *Notes of a Desolate Man* (Columbia University Press, 1999)

### SHORT STORIES

*Wuyan* 巫言 (2006). Translated by Howard Goldblatt and Sylvia Li-chun Lin as 'Witch's Brew', published in *Asymptote* (2012)

*Shijimo de Huali* 世紀末的華麗 (1990). Translated by Eva Hung as 'Fin de Siècle Splendour', published in *Running Wild: New Chinese Writers* (Columbia University Press, 1994)

*Roushen Pusa* 肉身菩薩 (1989). Translated by Fran Martin as 'Bodhisattva Incarnate', published in *Angelwings: Contemporary Queer Fiction from Taiwan* (University of Hawaii Press, 2003)

*Chai Shifu* 柴師父 (1988). Translated by Michelle Yeh as 'Master Chai', published in *Running Wild: New Chinese Writers* (Columbia University Press, 1994)

*Yanxia zhi Du* 炎夏之都 (1986). Translated by Michelle Yeh as 'A City of Hot Summer', published in *The Chinese Pen* (1988), also translated by Ellen Lai-shan Yeung as 'The Long Hot Summer', published in *Renditions 35/36* (1991)

### ESSAYS

*Women You Yiwu Chengwei Ling Yixie Ren* 我們有義務成為另一些人 2015, translated by Ping Zhu as 'We All Change into Somebody Else', published in *Chinese Literature Today* (2016)

AC

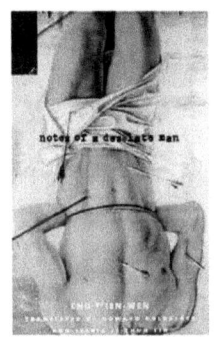

notes of a desolate man

CHU T'IEN-WEN

# SHARON CHUNG
鍾曉陽 [(1962– )]

Born in Guangdong Province, Chung immigrated to Hong Kong with her family when she was a toddler. Later, she studied in the United States before moving to Australia. Now she resides in San Francisco.

Chung started writing as a teenager and counts Eileen Chang, Taiwan campus romances, and the classic eighteenth century novel, *The Dream of the Red Chamber* (红楼梦, a.k.a. *The Story of the Stone*) as influences. Her first novel was *Pinwheel Without Wind* (停车暂借问, not translated), published in 1981 when she was only eighteen. Considered a modern classic, the novel is set during the Japanese occupation of Northeast China. The young protagonist falls in love with a doctor returning from Japan but their romance is cut short by the war. The story traces the life of the young woman into middle age. In 1996, Chung published her second novel, *Silent Truth* (遺恨傳奇, not translated), a re-telling of *The Dream of the Red Chamber*. Twenty-two years later, she revised the novel and re-titled it *Regrets* (遺恨, see below).

Sharon Chung enjoys reading her own work out loud

accompanied by music and is known for meticulously editing her books.

## Selected Works

So far, Chung's works have not been published in English translation. We understand that *Regrets* has been translated for Grayhawk Agency but has not yet found a publisher.

# DI AN
笛安 <sup>(1983- )</sup>

Li Di'an publishes under her given name Di An. She was born into a literary family from Taiyuan, Shanxi Province; both her parents are writers. Her first novel about young love, *Goodbye Paradise* (告别天堂), not translated), was published in 2005 when she was only twenty-one years old. The author also gave the Chinese edition an English name, *Ashes to Ashes*. Since then, she has published five novels and several novellas. She is a graduate of the Sorbonne and École des Hautes Etudes en Sciences Sociales (EHESS) in Paris. From 2010 to 2016, she was editor-in-chief of the literary magazine *ZUI Found* (文艺风赏).

Since she published her first novel, Di An's writings have developed from depicting fairytale-like stories to unveiling the tragic emotions behind the fairytales. She has won several major literary prizes in China, including 2015 Most Promising New Talent Award (人民文学新人奖) awarded by People's Literature Publishing House, and the People's Literature Novel Prize (人民文学奖) in 2018.

## Selected Works

SHORT STORIES

*Weilianmusi zhi mu* 威廉姆斯之墓 Translated by Alice Xin Liu as *Williams' Tomb*, in *Pathlight: New Chinese Writing* 1 (2011)

# DUNG KAI-CHEUNG
董啟章 <sup>(1967- )</sup>

Dung Kai-cheung was born in Hong Kong. He has an MPhil in Comparative Literature from the University of Hong Kong, and is an author, journalist, playwright and essayist. He is also a lecturer at the Chinese University of Hong Kong where he teaches Chinese writing. His major novels include *Histories of Time: The Lustre of Mute Porcelain* (時間繁史：啞瓷之光 , not translated), *Atlas: The Archæology of an Imaginary City* (地圖集———一個想像的城市的考古學) and *Exploitation of the Works of Nature* (天工开物，栩栩如真, not translated). He won the Hong Kong Arts Development Council Rookie Award in 1997, Hong Kong Art Development Award Best Artist of the Year (Literature) in 2008, and Best Translated Work Award-Science Fiction & Fantasy Translation Award (USA) in 2013. He was shortlisted for the Dream of the Red Chamber Award (HK) in both 2008 and 2020. His more recent books include *Loving Life* (*Aiqi* 爱妻 , not translated) and *Ordering Son* (*Minzi*命子, not translated).

## Selected Works

NOVELS

*Dituji—Yige Xiangxiang de Chengshi de Kaoguxue* 地圖集—— 一個
想像的城市的考古學 (2009) Translated by Dung Kai-cheung,
Anders Hansson and Bonnie McDougall as *Atlas: The Archæology of an
Imaginary City* (Columbia University Press, 2012)

SHORT STORIES

*Luan Ya* 乳牙. Translated by Nick Stember as *Crooked Teeth*, published
in *Ricepaper Magazine*, December 2016

BBS

# FANG FANG
方方 <sup>(1955-)</sup>

Fang Fang is the pen name of Wang Fang (汪芳). She was born into a literati family in Nanjing, Jiangsu Province, but the family moved to Wuhan when she was two years old. Before attending Wuhan University, she spent four years working as a stevedore in Wuhan to support her family; in interviews, she recalls this period as a formative time, which provided material for her early works such as *The View* (风景, not translated). Her empathic portraits of Wuhanese people, from factory workers to intellectuals, earned her recognition as a leading figure in the 'new realist literature' movement (新写实主义文学). According to the writer Han Shaogong (韩少功), the secret of Fang Fang's success is that she is able to capture the minutiae of ordinary life without losing its thread.

It is precisely Fang Fang's realism and her focus on individuals' experiences during major social changes that have made her works so controversial in China. The novel *Soft Burial* (软埋, not translated) teases out long-buried memories of a landowning family's suffering during the Land Reform Movement in the 1950s. Vehemently criticised

115

by leftists, the book was banned by the Chinese government in May 2017, despite having won the prestigious Luyao Literary Award (路遥文学奖) in 2016.

As a Wuhan-based author, Fang Fang posted sixty diary entries on the Chinese social media platform Weibo during the coronavirus outbreak from late January to March 2020, documenting the lockdown experience in the city of eleven million people. Portraying some negative aspects of the situation, her diaries attracted tremendous attention abroad following swift translation and publication in most major European languages, including English.

### Selected Works

NOVELLAS

*You Ai Wu Ai Doushi Mingxin Kegu* 有爱无爱都是铭心刻骨
(2012). Translated by Eleanor Goodman as 'Love and its Lack are Emblazoned on the Heart Forever', in *By the River: Seven Contemporary Chinese Novellas* (University of Oklahoma Press, 2016)

NON-FICTION

*Wuhan Riji* 武汉日记 (2020). Translated by Michæl Berry as *Wuhan Diary: Dispatches from a Quarantined City* (HarperVia, 2020)

CXXY

# FENG JICAI

冯骥才 [(1942– )]

Feng Jicai is known as a pioneer member of the Scar Literature movement that emerged from the Cultural Revolution. He was born in the northern port city of Tianjin, although his family was originally from Ningbo in Zhejiang Province. Feng Jicai began as a painter in the traditional Chinese style. During the Cultural Revolution, he started writing in secret. His writing career was launched with the 1979 publication of *The Carved Pipe* (雕花煙斗), a collection of short stories. Since then, he has published more than fifty stories, both long and short, fiction and non-fiction. In 2013, Feng Jicai won the 22nd Montblanc de la Culture Arts Patronage Award. In 2018, the China Federation of Literary and Art Circles honored Feng Jicai with a Lifetime Achievement Award in Folk Art and Literature. His best-known works include the *Three-Inch Golden Lotus* (三寸金蓮), *Ten Years of Madness* (一百個人的十年), and *Faces in the Crowd* (俗世奇人).

## Selected Works

NOVELS

*San Cun Jinlian* 三寸金莲 (1997). Translated by David Wakefield as *The Three-Inch Golden Lotus: A Novel on Foot Binding* (University of Hawai'I Press, 1994)

SHORT STORY COLLECTIONS
*Sushi Qiren* 俗世奇人 (2000). Translated by Olivia Milburn as *Faces in the Crowd: 36 Extraordinary Tales of Tianjin* (Sinoist Books, 2019)

NON-FICTION
*Yibai ge Ren de Shinian* 一百個人的十年 (1987). Translated by Denny Chiu, Deborah Cao, Lawrence Tedesco, and Cathy Silber as *Voices from the Whirlwind: an oral history of the Chinese Cultural Revolution* (Random House, 1991)

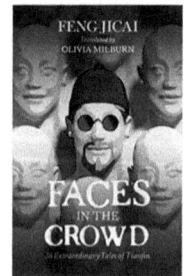

# FENG TANG
冯唐 <sup>(1971– )</sup>

Trained in medicine and business, Feng Tang branched out into literature to become the consummate chronicler of youth in Beijing, and one of the most controversial authors in China, best known for the erotic content of his novels.

His earliest trilogy of semi-autobiographical novels, written when the author was just eighteen years old – *Delight* (欢喜, Not translated), *Everything Grows* (万物生长, Not translated) and *Give me a Girl at Age Eighteen* (十八岁给我一个姑娘) – is deeply evocative of growing up in the Chinese capital during the 1990s.

In his more recent novels, Feng Tang delves into themes of love and sexual desire. In *One and Only* (不二), a titillating work set in the Tang dynasty, he employs a classical style harking back to the traditional racy novels of imperial China. The novel tells the story of Buddhist monks and nuns achieving enlightenment through unorthodox means. Written with the knowledge that it could not be published in Mainland China, *One and Only* went directly to publishing houses in Hong Kong and Taiwan and quickly became a bestseller.

His 2014 novel *Su Nü Jing* (素女经), set in the present, takes its title from a Han Dynasty erotic manual. Playing with elements of science fiction, Feng Tang tells the story of a middle-aged man's struggle to cope with his extramarital desires, which eventually lead him to develop a machine that can bring perfect sexual satisfaction and free humankind from romantic entanglements. A bowdlerized version of this novel was published in Mainland China a year later in 2015, under the title of *Nüshen Yihao* (女神一号).

### Selected Works

**NOVELS**

*Shiba Sui Gei Wo Yige Guniang* 十八岁给我一个姑娘 (2005). Translated by Anon as *Give me a Girl at Age Eighteen* (People's Literature Publishing House, 2018)

*Beijing Beijing* 北京北京 (2007) translated by Michelle Deeter as *Beijing Beijing* (Amazon Crossing, 2015)

**SHORT STORIES**

*Majiang* 麻将, translated by Brendan O'Kane as *Mahjong* (Read Paper Republic, 2015)

CXXY

# GAO XINGJIAN

高行健 (1940– )

Before he left China permanently in 1987, the 2000 Nobel Laureate in Literature Gao Xingjian was known on the mainland as a painter and playwright, not as an author of fiction. After graduating from the French Department at Beijing Foreign Studies University in 1962, he worked in Beijing as a French-to-Chinese translator. He once accompanied a group of Chinese authors including the literary giant Ba Jin (巴金) to Paris; it was this trip that inspired his essay 'Ba Jin in Paris' (巴金在巴黎). In 1985, he and the artist Yin Guangzhong (尹光中) held an exhibition of works in clay, which turned out to be the only exhibition Gao Xingjian would ever curate in mainland China.

Throughout the 1980s, Gao staged a number of experimental plays, most of which made their debut at the Beijing People's Art Theatre, including *Absolute Signal* 绝对信号), *Bus Stop* (车站) and *Wild Men* (野人). As the decade progressed, several of his works were banned from being performed in China, including *The Other Shore* (彼岸, 1986), but it was the publication of his political play *Escape* (逃亡), which makes reference to the Tiananmen Square protests, in 1990 that led to the definitive banning of all his works in China.

His famous novel *Soul Mountain* (灵山) and the subsequent *One Man's Bible* (一个人的圣经) were completed in France. Gao Xingjian won the Nobel Prize for Literature as a French citizen, and initial coverage of the award in Chinese media was quickly halted by the authorities, who denounced the award as 'politically motivated'. For all these reasons, Gao Xingjian is much less widely read in China than in the West.

### Selected Works

NOVELS

*Yige Ren de Shengjing* 一个人的圣经 (1999). Translated by Mabel Lee as *One Man's Bible* (Flamingo, 2002)

*Ling Shan* 灵山 (1990). Translated by Mabel Lee as *Soul Mountain* (Flamingo, 2000)

PLAYS

*Shan Hai Jingzhuan* 山海经传 (1992). Translated by Gilbert Fong as *Of Mountains and Seas* (Chinese University Press, 2008)

*Taowang* 逃亡 (1990). Translated by Gilbert Fong as *Escape* (Chinese University Press, 2007)

*Che Zhan* 车站 (1983). Translated by Carla Kirkwood as *Bus Stop*, in *World Anthology of Drama* (Longman, 2004)

*Bi'an* 彼岸 (1989). Translated by Gilbert Fong as *The Other Shore* (Chinese University Press, 2000)

POETRY

*Youshen Yu Xuansi* 遊神与玄思 (2012). Translated by Gibert Fong as *Wandering Mind and Metaphysical Thoughts* (Chinese University

Press, 2018)

SHORT STORY COLLECTION
*Buying a Fishing Rod for my Grandfather.* Translated by Mabel Lee
(Harper Perennial, 2010)

# GE FEI

格非 [(1964– )]

Ge Fei (real name, Liu Yong) is a winner of the prestigious Mao Dun Literature Prize and a professor of comparative literature at Tsinghua University. Inspired by Western modernist literature, Ge Fei established himself as an avant-garde writer with a string of experimental works in the 1980s, including his debut short story *Remembering Mr Wu You* (追忆乌攸先生), the novella *The Lost Boat* (迷舟) which brought him instant fame, and *Flock of Brown Birds* (褐色鸟群), a Borgesian novella deemed by some to be one of the most esoteric works in modern Chinese literature.

From the 1990s onwards, Ge Fei began to re-evaluate literary realism and dedicated seventeen years to his *Jiangnan Trilogy* (also known as the *Utopia* series). The trilogy is made up of *Peach Blossom Paradise* (人面桃花), *Rivers and Mountains in Dreams* (山河入梦), and *Southern Spring* (春尽江南) and tells the story of one family during three pivotal periods in modern Chinese history, from the 1911 Xinhai Revolution to the Maoist era and finally to present-day China.

## Selected Works

**NOVELS**

*Renmian Taohua* 人面桃花 (2004). Translated by Canaan Morse as *Peach Blossom Paradise* (New York Review of Books, 2020).

*Yinshen Yi* 隐身衣 (2012). Translated by Canaan Morse as *The Invisibility Cloak* (Penguin, 2016)

**NOVELLAS AND SHORT STORIES**

*Mi Zhou* 迷舟 (1987). Translated by Caroline Mason as *The Lost Boat*, in the multi-author collection of the same name (Wellsweep, 1993)

*Hese Niaoqun* 褐色鸟群 (1989). Translated by Poppy Toland as *Flock of Brown Birds* (Penguin Australia, 2016)

CXXY

# GUO JINGMING
郭敬明 (1983– )

A 'pop writer' and one of China's first internet celebrities, Guo Jingming has enjoyed huge commercial success with his novels and their film and TV spin-offs, and has several times been listed as China's highest-earning author.

Born in Sichuan, he first found fame while still in high school, when he won first prize in the New Concept Writing Competition, organized by seven top Chinese universities and the *Mengya* literary journal, in both 2001 and 2002. After moving to Shanghai, Guo published his first novel, *City of Fantasy* (also known as *Ice Fantasy*) (幻城), which became a bestseller. Critics, however, attacked him for narcissism and self-obsession – and in 2004, he was convicted and fined for plagiarism, relating to his second novel, *Never Flowers in Never Dreams* (梦里花落知多少). In December 2020, Guo apologized to Zhuang Yu, the author whose work he was found to have plagiarized, and pledged to set up an anti-plagiarism foundation. Despite such controversies, his novels have remained popular with the young generation, of whom he says, 'Today's young people don't understand life depicted by older authors. So they like my work because it's by a writer their age about stuff very close to their lives.' His three-part novel *Tiny Times* (小时代), about the lives and relationships of a group of young women in contemporary Shanghai, appeared between 2008 and 2014, and a series of four films of the same name came out between 2013 and 2015.

## Selected works

None of his works are currently available in English translation.

In Italian translation, *Linjie · Jueji* 临界 · 爵迹 (literally, Critical · Knight's Seal) was translated by R. Moratto as *Il Sigillo del Cavaliere* (Fanucci, 2012)

# HA JIN
哈金 (1956– )

Jin Xuefei Jin (金雪飞), better known under his pen name, Ha Jin, is a Chinese-American poet and novelist. His early education was interrupted when the Cultural Revolution closed schools in 1966. At the age of fourteen, he joined the People's Liberation Army (PLA) and served for five years. He then worked as a railway telegraph operator for three years, during which he learned English by listening to the radio. After the Cultural Revolution ended, he obtained an undergraduate degree in English at Heilongjiang University and a Masters degree in American Literature at Shandong University. In 1989, he was pursuing a PhD in American Literature at Brandeis University when the Tiananmen crackdown occurred. Writing for the *New York Times*, he states that the events 'shocked me so much that for weeks I was in a daze'. They also spurred his decision to 'go the way of Conrad and Nabokov', and he now writes exclusively in English.

Ha Jin starting publishing poetry, but it was his short story collection *Ocean of Words* that won him the PEN/ Hemingway award in 1997. In 1999, his first full-length novel *Waiting* was awarded the PEN/Faulkner Award and the National Book Award in the United States. His stories often take place between China and the United States and deal with themes such as immigration and exile. Despite being a renowned writer in the United States, the sensitivity of his subject matter makes most of his work unpublishable in China, although Chinese versions of many of his books are available in Hong Kong and Taiwan.

## Selected Works

NOVELS

*A Song Everlasting: A Novel* (Pantheon, 2021)
*The Boat Rocker* (Center Point, 2017)
*A Map of Betrayal* (2014) (Vintage, 2015)
*Nanjing Requiem: A Novel* (Vintage, 2012)
*A Free Life* (Vintage, 2009)
*The Crazed* (Vintage, 2004)
*War Trash* (Vintage, 2005)
*Waiting: A Novel* (Vintage, 2000)
*In the Pond* (Vintage, 2000)

PŒTRY

*A Distant Center* (Copper Canyon Press, 2018)
*Wreckage* (Hanging Loose Press, 2001)
*Facing Shadows* (Hanging Loose Press, 1996)
*Between Silences: A Voice from China* (University of Chicago Press, 1990)

SHORT STORY COLLECTIONS

*A Good Fall* (Vintage, 2010)
*The Bridegroom* (Vintage, 2001)
*Under the Red Flag* (Steerforth Press, 1999)

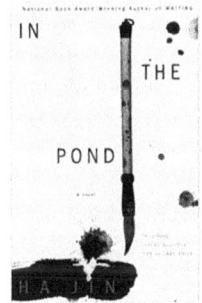

# HAI YAN

海宴 <sup>(dates unknown)</sup>

Hai Yan burst onto the online fiction scene in 2006 with the *wuxia* (martial arts) novel *Nirvana in Fire* (琅琊榜), which is set in the fourth century interregnum period between the Northern Wei dynasty and the Southern Liang dynasty. In 2007, Blossom Press published the first part of the book in print. In 2011, the second part was published by Sichuan Literature and Art Publishing House, followed by the third part in 2014. In 2015, Hai Yan wrote the screenplay for the TV adaptation, which became one of the biggest commercial successes at the time and was critically well received.

Hai Yan is a pseudonym and the author has never given any face-to-face interviews. According to her publisher, Hai Yan studied English at university, and loves literature and history. She is a self-described introvert who loves cooking and traveling. She was born in Chengdu in Sichuan Province, started writing in high school and continued writing while working for a real estate company.

## Selected Works

Hai Yan's books have not been translated, but the series *Nirvana in Fire* is available on Netflix and Youtube.

# HAN DONG
韩东 (1961– )

When Han Dong's parents were banished to the countryside during the Cultural Revolution, they took their eight-year-old son with them. He did not return to the city until the Cultural Revolution ended in 1976, and this rural childhood later became the source of inspiration for many of his works. In 1982, he graduated from Shandong University with a degree in philosophy, and subsequently taught in Xi'an and Nanjing before becoming an independent writer in 1993.

Han Dong took up poetry in his university days and began publishing in the 1980s. In 1985, he co-founded the poetry magazine *Them* (他们), which became an important platform for avant-garde 'Third Generation Poets' (第三代诗人). In 1998, he and the writer and director Zhu Wen (朱文) challenged the literary establishment by publishing the (in)famous 'Fracture Questionnaire' (断裂问卷), which contained negative opinions of established literary figures written by fifty-six writers. This came to be seen as a young generation's call for a new direction in literature.

Han Dong is best-known and has been most influential as a poet. However, he also has a considerable corpus of essays, short stories, novellas and full-length novels, the first of was *Banished* (扎根, 2003). This was followed by *The Metamorphosis of the Sent-down Youth* (知青变形记, not translated) and *Small Town Handsome Guy* (小城好汉之英特迈往, not translated), all of which deal with the experience of youths sent down to the countryside during the Cultural Revolution.

Han Dong places a particular emphasis on colloquial (民间) language, and his fiction and essays, like his poetry, are noted for being deliberately plain, spare and precise, as well as wryly humorous.

## Selected works

**NOVELS**

*Zha Gen* 扎根 (2003) translated by Nicky Harman as *Banished! A Novel* (UH Press, 2009)

**NOVELLAS, SHORT STORIES AND ESSAYS**

*Chuang Jing* 窗景. Translated by Nicky Harman as 'View from a Window' (Read Paper Republic [https://paper-republic.org/pubs/read/], 2020)

*You You Lu Ming* 呦呦鹿鸣. Translated by Nicky Harman as 'The Cry of the Deer', (Read Paper Republic, 2016)

*Huahua Chuan Qi* 花花传奇. Translated by Nicky Harman as *A Tabby Cat's Tale* (Frisch, 2016)

*Ci Dai Yi Si* 此呆已死. Translated by Nicky Harman as 'This Moron is Dead' in *Shi Cheng: Stories from Urban China* (Comma Press, 2012)

*Zhan Xin Shi* 崭新世. Translated by Helen Wang and Nicky Harman as 'Brand-New World' (Paper Republic, 2012)

*Jia Fa* 假发. Translated by Philip Hand as 'The Wig' (Granta, October 2012)

*Lai zi Da Lian de Dianhua* 来自大连的电话. *A Phone Call from Dalian* (Zephyr Press, 2012). Various translators.

# HAN SHAOGONG

**韩少功** (1953–)

In 1968, fifteen-year-old Han Shaogong signed up to 'go down' to the countryside during the Cultural Revolution, and subsequently spent the next decade in the town of Miluo, Hunan Province. He was born in the city of Changsha, also in Hunan Province. He began publishing short stories after the Cultural Revolution ended, and in 1985 he published an essay called *The Roots of Literature* (文学的根, not translated) to promote 'root-seeking literature' (寻根文学), which sought to rediscover traditional cultural identities through close observation of rural communities. Like the earlier writer Shen Congwen (沈从文, 1902–1988), Han Shaogong has a strong interest in the mystical traditions that set Hunan and its people apart from the rest of China. He spent many years searching within Hunan's ancient traditions for an alternative to China's mainstream Han culture.

Han Shaogong is best known for his magical realist novellas, such as *Pa Pa Pa* (爸爸爸), *Woman Woman Woman* (女女女) and his full-length novel *A Dictionary of Maqiao* (马桥词典 *Maqiao Cidian*). The latter assumes the form of a dictionary containing 115 interconnected entries on life in the fictitious village of Maqiao (based on the real town of Miluo), which are compiled by a young student sent to the countryside during the Cultural Revolution. Han Shaogong also documented some of his first-hand observations of contemporary rural life in the collection of essays *Southside of the Mountain, Northside of the Water* (山南水北, not translated), which was written in the early 2000s when he returned to Miluo and set up home there.

## Selected Works

**NOVELS**

*Maqiao Cidian* 马桥词典 (1996). Translated by Julia Lovell as *A Dictionary of Maqiao* (Columbia University Press, 2003)

**SHORT STORIES**

*Shan Ge Tian Shang Lai* 山歌天上来 (2006). Translated by Lucas Klein as 'Mountain Songs from the Heavens', collected in *By the River: Seven Contemporary Chinese Novellas* (University of Oklahoma Press, 2016)

*Mo Ri* 末日 (2007). Translated by Bruce Humes as 'Doomsday' (*Pathlight*, 2013)

**SHORT STORY COLLECTIONS**

*Guiqulai* 归去来. Translated by Martha Cheung as *Homecoming? And Other Stories* (*Renditions*, 1995). The collection includes the following short stories:

*Guiqulai* 归去来. Translated as 'Homecoming'
*Lan Gaizi* 蓝盖子. Translated as 'The Blue Bottle-cap'
*Ba Ba Ba* 爸爸爸. Translated as 'Pa Pa Pa'
*Nü Nü Nü* 女女女. Translated as 'Woman Woman Woman'

# HAN SONG
韩松 <sup>(1965–)</sup>

A journalist at China's official Xinhua news agency by day and a science fiction writer by night, Han Song is one of China's best-known and most prolific authors in a genre that until recently received little attention or respect within the country. In his capacity as a state-sanctioned journalist, Han Song has seen much and been allowed to say little, yet his observations and reflections go into his fiction. He is a writer who has managed to preserve his sense of wonder, particularly about all things technological, and to develop a finely-honed sense of social justice. Cloning and psychological manipulation are themes that regularly crop up in his writing – which soon makes clear that science fiction is merely a slightly warped mirror with which to reflect modern Chinese society.

Born in the city of Chongqing, Han Song is a multiple recipient of the Milky Way Prize (银河奖), China's highest profile sci-fi prize, and is regularly cited by younger writers as an influence on their work. He has authored dozens of short stories, published individually as well as in collections such as *Gravestone of the Universe* (宇宙墓碑, not translated),

which was written when he was a university student.
His best-known novels include *Red Ocean* (红色海洋, not
translated) about life after a nuclear apocalypse, *Mars Shines
on America* (火星照耀美国 , not translated ) about a Go player
in a virtual world run by a supercomputer, and *Subway* (地铁
, not translated), composed of five interconnected mystery
stories that take place in a subway.

## Selected Works

SHORT STORIES

*Tianxia zhi Shui* 天下之水 (2002). Translated by Anna Holmwood as
'All the Water in the World' in *Peregrine* (2011)

*Changcheng* 长城 (2003). Translated by Nathaniel Isaacson as 'The
Great Wall' in *Chinese Literature Today* volume 7 (2018)

*Chengke yu Chuangzaozhe* 乘客与创造者 (2005). Translated by
Nathaniel Isaacson as 'The Passengers and the Creator' in *The
Reincarnated Giant: An Anthology of Twenty-First-Century Chinese Science
Fiction* (Columbia University Press, 2018)

*Zaisheng Zhuan* 再生砖 (2010). Translated by Theodore Huters as
'Regenerated Bricks' in *The Reincarnated Giant: An Anthology of Twenty-
First-Century Chinese Science Fiction* (Columbia University Press, 2018)

*Shijie Shi Pingde* 世界是平的 (2011). Translated by Nathaniel Isaacson
as 'Earth Is Flat' in *Chinese Literature Today* volume 7 (2018)

*Mo Ban Ditie* 末班地铁 (1988). Translated by Jœl Martinsen as 'The
Last Subway' in *Pathlight* (Winter, 2012)

*Ditie Jingbian* 地铁惊变 (2011). Translated by Rachel Faith as 'Subway
Alarm' in the *Anthill* (2013)

*Mang Wanle* 忙完了 (2012). Translated by Nick Stember as 'Finished'
in *Los Angeles Review of Books China Channel* (2017)

*Yuzhou de Benxing* 宇宙的本性 (2013). Translated by Nathaniel
Isaacson as 'The Fundamental Nature of the Universe' in *Chinese
Literature Today* volume 7 (2018)

*An Jian* 安检 (2014). Translated by Ken Liu as 'Security Check' in
*Clarkesworld* (2015)

*Qianting* 潜艇 (2014). Translated by Ken Liu as 'Submarines' in
*Broken Stars: Contemporary Chinese Science Fiction* (Tor, 2019)

*Sailinge yu Chaoxianren* 塞林格与朝鲜人 (2016). Translated by Ken
Liu as 'Salinger and the Koreans' in *Broken Stars: Contemporary Chinese
Science Fiction* (Tor, 2019)

*Yinshen Quan* 隐身权 (2017). Translated by Ken Liu as 'The Right
to Be Invisible' in *Glossolalia: We Agree on Nothing: New Writing from
China* (PenAmerica, 2017)

*Liangzhi Xiaoniao* 两只小鸟 (1988). Translated by John Chu as 'Two
Small Birds' in *The Big Book of Science Fiction: The Ultimate Collection*
(Vintage Crime, 2016)

CXXY

# HAO JINGFANG

郝景芳 [(1984– )]

Born in Tianjin, Hao Jingfang is a science fiction writer, economist and social entrepreneur. In high school, she won first prize in the national New Concept writing competition and went on to study Physics at Tsinghua University, followed by a PhD in Economics.

She works as an economist at the China Development Research Foundation and is concerned with economic and educational inequality in China. She has set up a social enterprise in the area of child education, seeking to promote a liberal education for all children and special free educational programmes for poor children in mountain areas in China.

Hao Jingfang's fiction has appeared in various publications including *Mengya*, *Science Fiction World* and *ZUI Found*. She has published two full-length novels, *Vagabonds* (流浪苍穹, 2015) and *Return to Charon* (回到卡戎, 2012); a book of cultural essays, *Europe in Time*, and the short story collection *Star Travellers*.

In 2016 she became the first Chinese woman (and only second Chinese author) to win a highly prestigious Hugo award for her novella *Folding Beijing*.

## Selected Works

### NOVELS

*Liulang Cangqiong* 流浪苍穹 (2016). Translated by Ken Liu as *Vagabonds* (Head of Zeus, 2020)

### NOVELLA

*Beijing Zhedie* 北京折叠 (2015). Translated by Ken Liu as *Folding Beijing* (*Uncanny* magazine, 2015)

### SHORT STORIES

*Kanbujian de Xingqiu* 看不见的星球. Translated by Ken Liu as 'Invisible Planets', in the anthology *Invisible Planets* (Tor Books, 2016)
*Zuihou Yige Yonggan De Ren* 最后一个勇敢的人. Translated by Poppy Toland as 'The Last Brave Man' (*Pathlight* magazine, Spring 2013)

# HON LAI CHU
韓麗珠 <sup>(1978– )</sup>

Born in 1978 in Hong Kong, Hon Lai Chu began writing at the age of ten. With an absurdist gaze on the modern world that often prompts comparisons with Kafka, she invites her readers into gradually warping realities. She finished her first short story, 'The Water Pipe Forest' (輸水管森林, not translated), while still in middle school. Hon Lai Chu is the author of several novels, including *Grey Flower* (灰花, not translated), *The Kite Family* (風箏家族, 2015), *Body-sewing* (縫身, not translated) and *The Border of Centrifugation* (離心帶, not translated), as well as several collections of short stories. Her 2006 novel *The Kite Family* was selected as one of 2008's Books of the Year by the *China Times* in Taiwan. In 2004, she was awarded the Hong Kong Biennial Award for Chinese Literature (Fiction) for her short story collection *Silent Creature* (寧靜獸, not translated). In 2012, Hon Lai Chu co-authored the short story collection *A Dictionary of Two Cities* (雙城辭典, not translated) with Dorothy Tse, which won the Hong Kong Book Prize the following year. Her most recent work of fiction is the 2015 short story collection *Lost Caves* (失去洞穴, not translated).

## Selected Works

NOVELS

*Fengzheng Jiazu* 風箏家族 (2008). Translated by Andrea Lingenfelter as *The Kite Family* (Hong Kong University Press, 2015)

SHORT STORIES

*Yifu Yu* 遺腹語. Translated by Andrea Lingenfelter as 'Stolen Language in the Womb' (in *Tales of Our Time*, Guggenheim Museum Publications, 2016)

*Piao Ma* 飄馬. Translated by Andrea Lingenfelter as 'Puma' (Words Without Borders, 2018)

*Mu Ou* 木偶. Translated by Karen Curtis as 'Dummies' (Read Paper Republic, 2016)

ESSAYS

*Kanjian Taren* 看見他人. Translated by Andrea Lingenfelter as 'Hong Kong's Sickness' (Los Angeles Review of Books, China Channel, 2019)

AG

# HONG YING

虹影 [(1962– )]

The Chongqing-born British-Chinese novelist and poet Hong Ying is known internationally and loved by many for her raw honesty and intense emotionality. Hong Ying's most famous works include her autobiographical novel *Daughter of the River* (饥饿的女儿) and its sequel *Good Children of the Flower* (好儿女花). Both novels are based on her unhappy childhood as an illegitimate child in a poor family as well as the difficulties she faced in her first marriage. The latter took her to London in 1991, but she returned to China in 2004 after her divorce. She later met the English businessman and novelist Adam Williams and they married in 2009. She currently divides her time between London and Beijing.

Hong Ying is frequently perceived as a feminist advocate. The novel *K: The Art of Love* (K: 英国情人) is an imaginary account based on the real-life love affair between the English poet (and nephew of Virginia Woolf) Julian Bell and the Chinese author Ling Shuhua (凌叔华) in the 1930s. *The Concubine of Shanghai* (上海王 *Shanghai Wang*), a novel set in Shanghai in the early 1900s, tells the story of a prostitute called Cassia, whose relationships with three triad bosses eventually makes her the most powerful figure in the Shanghai underworld.

Hong Ying has also penned a series of five fantasy novels for her daughter, each book focusing on a magical adventure of a boy called Sangsang (神奇少年桑桑). The series has been published in a Chinese-English bilingual edition, with translations by Nicholas Smith and illustrations by Cherry Denman.

## Selected Works

NOVELS AND NON-FICTION

*Hao Ernü Hua* 好儿女花 (*Good Children of the Flower*). Translated by Gary Xu, Shelly Bryant, Nick Brown (Amazon Crossing, 2016)

*Shanghai Wang* 上海王 (2016). Translated by Liu Hong as *The Concubine of Shanghai* (Penguin, 2011)

*Kongque de Jiaohan* 孔雀的叫喊 (2003). Translated by Mark Smith and Henry Zhao as *Peacock Cries* (Marion Boyars, 2004)

*K: Yingguo Qingren* K: 英国情人 (2001). Translated by Nicky Harman and Henry Zhao as *K: The Art of Love* (Marion Boyars, 2002; Viking, 2011)

*Ji'e de Nü'er* 饥饿的女儿 (1997). Translated by Howard Goldblatt as *Daughter of the River: An Autobiography* (Grove Press, 2000)

# JIA PINGWA

贾平凹 (1952–)

Jia Pingwa was born in Dihua village (棣花镇), Danfeng county (丹凤县) in Shaanxi province and is one of the most prolific living authors in China today. In the mid-1970s, Jia moved from Dihua village to Xi'an, the capital of Shaanxi, to attend university. During the 1980s, he was influenced by the roots-seeking movement and wrote stories set in rural Shaanxi. In 1993, Jia published his most famous novel *Ruined City: A Novel* (废都), which was banned the same year due to its explicit sexual content. The fallout from the novel's reception caused many issues in Jia's personal life, including illness and the breakdown of his first marriage. However, the ban also increased his fame, and for years, copies of *Ruined City* sold for large sums of money on the black market. In 2009, he won the Mao Dun prize for his novel *Shaanxi [or Qin] Opera* (秦腔). The same year, the ban on *Ruined City* was lifted, and Jia is now a significant figure in China's cultural scene.

Many of Jia's works explore dark themes and the chasm between life in the city and life in the countryside. *Ruined City* follows a group of literary rivals in Xi'an and their attempts to undermine the most successful of the group, a lothario named Zhuang Zhidie. *Qin Opera* is a 600-page epic set in a Shaanxi village, recounting the story of a poor man in love with a married woman. The novel depicts village life in detail, as two families attempt to exert influence over the community. *Happy* (高兴) features Happy Liu – a migrant worker who moves to Xi'an to track down the recipient of his donated kidney but ends up finding love. Jia's 2016 novel *Broken Wings* (极花) is a story of human trafficking and the gender imbalance in rural parts of China where men outnumber women – a consequence of the One Child Policy. His most recent work, *The Sojourn Teashop* (暂坐), however, is set entirely in the city and has as its protagonists a group of women friends who find themselves enmeshed in political corruption even as they struggle to find personal fulfillment. Many of Jia's works are influenced by classical Chinese novels, such as *The Dream of the Red Chamber* and *The Golden Lotus* (金瓶梅).

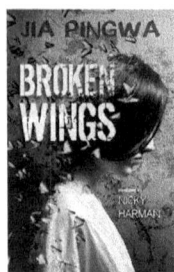 

# Selected Works

NOVELS

*Qinqiang* 秦腔 (2005). Translated as *Shaanxi [or Qin] Opera* [working title] by Nicky Harman and Dylan Levi King (Amazon Crossing, forthcoming 2023)

*Zan Zuo* 暂坐 (2020). Translated as *The Sojourn Teashop* [working title] by Nicky Harman and Liu Jun (ACA Publishing, forthcoming 2022)

*Lao Sheng* 老生 (2014). Translated as *The Mountain Whisperer* by Christopher Payne (ACA Publishing, 2021)

*Jihua* 极花 (2016). Translated as *Broken Wings* by Nicky Harman (ACA Publishing, 2019)

*Tu Men* 土门 (1996). Translated as *The Earthen Gate* by Hu Longfeng and He Longping (Valley Press, 2018)

*Dai Deng* 带灯 (2013). Translated as *The Lantern Bearer: A Novel* by Carlos Rojas (*CN Times*, Inc., 2017)

*Gaoxing* 高兴 (2007). Translated as *Happy Dreams* by Nicky Harman (Amazon Crossing, 2017)

*Feidu* 废都 (1993). Translated as *Ruined City: A Novel* by Howard Goldblatt (University of Oklahoma Press, 2016)

*Fuzao* 浮躁 (1987). Translated as *Turbulence* by Howard Goldblatt (Louisiana State Press, 1987)

NOVELLAS

*Daoliuhe* 倒流河 Translated as 'Backflow River' by Nicky Harman (Read Paper Republic, 2016)

AC

158

# JIN YONG
金庸 (1924–2018)

Jin Yong (pen name of Louis Cha, a.k.a. Cha Leung Yung 查良鏞), was born in 1924 in Haining, Zhejiang Province and worked as a translator and journalist in Shanghai throughout his young adult life. But it was in Hong Kong that he made his name, eventually becoming the city's most famous post-war writer. After being transferred there in 1948 for work, he continued working as a journalist, and later became a co-founder and editor-in-chief of the influential Chinese-language newspaper, *Ming Pao* (明报). But he also began writing his first stories of martial arts and knight errantry (*wuxia*) fiction, which appeared in serialised form in Hong Kong newspapers.

Jin Yong wrote his fifteen *wuxia* novels and novellas, which have wowed hundreds of millions of people worldwide, between 1955 and 1972, when he retired from writing to dedicate his time to editing and revising them, with the goal of releasing definitive editions. All of his novels have since been adapted into films, TV shows and radio dramas in Hong Kong, Taiwan and China.

One of the distinctive features of all of his novels is their ability to transcend typical distinctions of high- and lowbrow, as well as the geographical and ideological barriers that may have prevented earlier Hong Kong writers from achieving similar success throughout the Chinese-speaking world and beyond. Even periods of being banned in both Taiwan and mainland China for his criticisms of the Nationalist and Communist governments (an outspokenness he had practised since his youth, when he was expelled from high school for denouncing the then-Nationalist government) could not prevent him becoming the best-selling Chinese author of all time.

Jin Yong's novels have been translated into many languages. Four volumes of *Legend of the Condor Heroes* (widely considered his magnum opus) have recently appeared in *English: A Hero Born, A Bond Undone, A Snake Lies Waiting* and *A Heart Divided*. More titles are forthcoming.

## Selected Works

NOVELS

*She Diao Yingxiong Zhuan* 射鵰英雄传 (*Legend of the Condor Heroes*, 1957–59). Translated in four volumes: the first by Anna Holmwood as *A Hero Born* (MacLehose Press, 2018); the second by Gigi Chang as *A Bond Undone* (MacLehose Press, 2019); the third by Anna Holmwood and Gigi Chang as *A Snake Lies Waiting* (MacLehose Press, 2020); and the fourth by Gigi Chang and Shelly Bryant as *A Heart Divided* (MacLehose Press, 2021)

*Shu Jian Enchou Lu* 书剑恩仇录 (1955–56). Translated by Graham Earnshaw as *The Book and the Sword* (Oxford University Press, 2019)

*Lu Ding Ji* 鹿鼎记 (1969–72). Translated in three volumes by John Minford as *The Deer and the Cauldron*, Books 1, 2, and 3 (Oxford University Press, 1997, 2000, and 2003)

*Xueshan Feihu* 雪山飞狐. Translated by Olivia Mok as *Fox Volant of the Snowy Mountain* (The Chinese University of Hong Kong Press, 2020)

# LI ANG

# 李昂 (1952– )

Li Ang is the pen name of Shih Shu-tuan(施淑端), one of Taiwan's most prominent contemporary authors. Born in Lukang, Taiwan, she started writing fiction in middle school and launched her literary career at the age of sixteen with the publication of *Flower Season* (花季), a ground-breaking short story about an adolescent girl's sexual fantasies. After graduating in philosophy from Taiwan's Chinese Culture University, Li Ang studied drama at the University of Oregon before returning to teach at her *alma mater* and working as a columnist and short story writer.

Li Ang has addressed a wide range of subjects in her career, but she is best known for her candid and idiosyncratic portrayal of sexuality and gender politics. Her most iconic works are the three novels that make up the Taiwanese Trilogy, and document Taiwanese women's roles in a century of societal changes. *The Butcher's Wife* (殺夫), set in rural Taiwan in the early twentieth century, is a shocking exposition of a woman who is crushed by traditional patriarchy and eventually murders her abusive husband. The novel *Lost Garden* (迷園) is both a tale of an aristocratic woman's courtship of a nouveau riche playboy and a history of modern Taiwan, seen through the vicissitudes of her family's sumptuous garden. *Autobiography: A Novel* (自傳の小說, not translated) steps back in time to revisit the life of Hsieh Hsueh-hung (謝雪紅), a political heroine in Taiwan who fought against Japanese colonialists, the corruption of the Kuomintang (Nationalist government), and the totalitarianism of the Chinese Communist Party.

Her more recent works continue to explore sex, power, and politics in contemporary Taiwan.

## Selected Works

NOVELS

*Shafu: Lucheng gushi* 殺夫: 鹿城故事 (1983). Translated by Howard Goldblatt and Ellen Yeung as *The Butcher's Wife* (Peter Owen Publishing, 2002)

*Mi Yuan* 迷園 (1991). Translated by Sylvia Li-chun Lin and Howard Goldblatt as *The Lost Garden* (Columbia University Press, 2015)

SHORT STORIES

*Huaji* 花季 (1968). Translated by Howard Goldblatt as 'Flower Season', collected in *Bamboo Shoots After the Rain: Contemporary Stories by Women Writers of Taiwan* (The Feminist Press at The City University of New York, 1990)

*Niurou Mian* 牛肉面. Translated by Sylvia Li-chun Lin as 'Beef Noodles' in *Chinese Literature Today* volume 9 (2011)

*You Quxian de Wawa* 有曲线的娃娃. Translated by Howard Goldblatt as 'Curvaceous Dolls' in *A Place of One's Own: Stories of Self in China* (Oxford University Press,1987)

*Yi Feng Weiji de Qingshu* 一封未寄的情書 (1989). Translated by Howard Goldblatt as 'A Love Letter Never Sent' in *Worlds of Modern*

*Chinese Fiction* (Armonk, 1991)

*Dai Zhencao Dai de Mogui* 戴贞操带的魔鬼. Translated by Laura Jane Way as 'The Devil in a Chastity Belt' in *The Chinese Pen* magazine (当代台湾文学英译, 2000)

# LI ER
李洱 <sup>(1966– )</sup>

Li Er was born in Henan province, and has emerged since the 2000s as a critically acclaimed pioneer in the field of Chinese literature. Though he has published a large number of short stories which have appeared in mainland literary journals such as *Zuojia* (作家), *Shouhuo* (收获), *Dajia* (大家), *Renmin Wenxue* (人民文学), *Shanhua* (山花), *Shidai Wenxue* (时代文学), to date, he has only written three full length novels: *Coloratura* (花腔, sometimes referred to in English by the title *Truth and Variations*), *Cherry on a Pomegranate* (石榴树上结樱桃) and his most recent novel, *Brother Yingwu* (应物兄 not translated). This trilogy, however, represents the defining publication of Li's career thus far. The most recent volume, *Brother Yingwu*, took Li thirteen years to write; and in 2019 it was awarded the prestigious Mao Dun Literature Prize – a recognition that cements Li's current position as a commanding voice in China's literary world.

Li's works are historically informed. He not only sets many of his stories in various moments of China's past, but he also repackages historical narrative styles for a contemporary audience. He wrote Coloratura in the style of a Qing novel, whilst *Brother Yingwu* draws inspiration from the narrative style of the Confucian classics.

Aside from writing, Li also works at the National Museum for Modern Chinese Literature in Beijing. In addition to *Coloratura*, a number of his short stories have also been published in translation, including a 2016 translation of 'Forgetting' (遗忘) by Annelise Finegan Wasmoen in *The White Review*.

## Selected Works

**NOVELS**

*Hua Qiang* 花腔 (2001). Translated as Coloratura by Jeremy Tiang (University of Ohio Press, 2019)

**SHORT STORY**

*Yiwang* 遗忘 (2016). Translated as 'Forgetting' by Annelise Finegan Wasmœn, published in *The White Review*, January 2016

AC

# LI JINGRUI
## 李静睿

Li Jingrui was a journalist reporting on legal affairs in China for eight years, before her resignation in 2012. She then turned to other forms of writing, including her own column in the Chinese edition of The Wall Street Journal. She now concentrates mostly on writing fiction. She has published a collection of short stories, *Tales of a Small Town* (小城故事), and a novel, *Small Town Girl* (小镇姑娘), in which she sensitively explores human emotions and human fate. Her stories tackle a range of topics, including the everyday lives of ordinary people in a small town in Sichuan and students exiled in New York after Tian'anmen. Her latest works include the short story collection *North Boulevard* (北方大道), a collection of essays, *Another World of Yesterday* (死于昨日世界), and the novel *Tiny Destiny* (微小的命运).

## Selected Works

ESSAYS

*Aiqing, Yige Juedingxing Shunjian* 爱情，一个决定性瞬间. Translated by Anne Henochowicz as *Love, A Decisive Moment* (*China Digital Times*, February 23, 2016)

*Wo xiangxin hui you yi ke songdiao de luosi* 我相信会有一颗松掉的螺丝钉. Translated by Luisetta Mudie as *One Day, One of the Screws will Come Loose* (*Read Paper Republic*, June 16, 2016)

SHORT STORIES

*Xiaocheng* 小城. Translated by Helen Wang as 'Small Town' (*Los Angeles Review of Books, China Channel*, October 5, 2018)

*Shizong* 失踪. Translated by Helen Wang as 'Missing' (*Read Paper Republic*, August 6, 2015)

*Chenmo de Dongtian* 沉默的冬天. Translated by Nicholas Richards as 'A Quiet Winter' (*The World of Chinese*, October 5, 2015)

FB

# LI PIK-WAH / LI BIHUA
# (LILIAN LEE)

李碧華 [(1959– )]

Li Pi-Hua was born in 1959 as Li Pak (李白), and is also known as Lil[l]ian Lee, and Lee Pik-wah. She is a prolific Hong Kong novelist, screenwriter, and reporter. Lee's writing is known for blending traditional Chinese, supernatural, and everyday Hong Kong elements into her narratives. Her works such as *Rouge* (胭脂扣, not translated), *Farewell My Concubine* (霸王別姬, 1994) and *Green Snake* (青蛇, not translated) were adapted into films in the late '80s and early '90s to great international acclaim – *Farewell My Concubine* won many prestigious film awards, including a Palme d'Or and a Golden Globe. Lee also co-wrote the screenplay for all the adoptions. Her 2005 screenplay *Dumpling* (餃子) was nominated for Best Screenplay at the Hong Kong Film Awards. Lee trained in traditional Chinese dance when she was young and, under her direction, several of her novels have been adapted as dance dramas. One of Hong Kong's best-selling authors, Lee has published twenty-eight novels, fourteen screenplays, and dozens of essays. Yet while her most famous novels, such as *Farewell*

*My Concubine* and *The Last Princess of Manchuria* (滿洲國妖
艷—川島芳子, 1997), have been published in English, many
of her other popular novels like her 2007 *Life and Death
Bridge* (生死桥) have not yet been translated.

## Selected Works

NOVELS

*Bawang Bie Ji* 霸王別姬. Translated by Andrea Lingenfelter as
*Farewell My Concubine* (Harper Perennial, 1994)
*Manzhouguo Yaoyan-Chuandao Fangzi* 滿洲國妖艷—川島芳子.
Translated by Andrea Kelly as *The Last Princess of Manchuria* (William
Morrow and Co, 1997)

SCREENPLAYS

*Yanzhi Kou* 胭脂扣. *Rouge,* 1995 US Release
*You Seng* 诱僧. *Temptation of a Monk,* 1995 US Release
*Bawang Bie Ji* 霸王別姬. *Farewell My Concubine,* 1993 US Release

AG

# LIN BAI
# 林白 <sup>(1958–)</sup>

Lin Bai was born in Guangxi and currently splits her time between Beijing and Wuhan. Since the beginning of her career in the mid-1990s, Lin has published twenty-four novels and novellas, along with seven essay collections. She writes fiction that spotlights women's voices and is particularly renowned for her portrayal of women's sexuality. This is especially true of Lin's breakout 1994 work, *A War of One's Own* (一个人的战争, not translated). The success of *A War of One's Own* established Lin as one of the foremost writers of women's fiction in China. Her work has been recognised by a number of China's literary awards. In 1998, Lin won the first Chinese Women's Prize for Fiction. In 2005, she won a Chinese Literature Media Prize and was named Novelist of the Year for her novel, *The Words of Village Wives* (妇女闲聊绿, not translated). In August 2014, Lin was awarded the prestigious Lao She Literary Award for her 2013 novel, *Chronicles of My Life in the North* (北去来辞, not translated).

*A War of One's Own*, *The Words of Village Wives*, and *Chronicles of My Life in the North* are Lin's best-known works to date. Each explores women's voices in different ways, and are at times autobiographical. *A War of One's Own* tells the story of a young girl moving from a southern province to Beijing, and her journey of emotional and sexual self-discovery. *The Words of Village Wives* is almost like an oral history, lacing together interviews and fictional conversations with women living in a rural village. Lin describes the book as conveying the 'voices of real people.'

## Selected Works

**POETRY**

*Lockdown Poems: The Road to the Crematorium*, translated by David Haysom, in *Read Paper Republic: Epidemic*, 2020

AC

# LIU CIXIN
## 刘慈欣 (1963– )

Liu Cixin was born in Shanxi and is one of China's most famous science fiction authors. In the late 1990s, Liu left his career as an engineer to pursue writing. The short stories he wrote during this period consistently received Galaxy awards for science fiction. However, it was his first novel *The Three Body Problem* (三体) that really established Liu in China's literary scene. The novel was the first of a trilogy, *Remembrance of Earth's Past* (地球往事), which has become Liu' s most influential set of works to date. Since the publication of Ken Liu (no relation)'s English translation of *The Three Body Problem*, which was awarded a Hugo Award in 2014, Liu has received widespread international recognition. He and his works have been the subject of multiple articles in *The New Yorker*, *The Paris Review* and other publications, and he can count Barack Obama as one of his fans.

Liu's work often combines classic science fiction tropes with details from China's cultural and political history. The *Remembrance* trilogy relates an epic struggle between humanity and a group of alien invaders called Trisolarians from the planet Trisolaris. Many of his plots also revolve around an ominous countdown; in his 2000 novella *The Wandering Earth* (流浪地球), humans attempt to prevent a collision between Earth and other planets, whilst his most recent work *The Golden Plains* (黄金原野) published in 2018, features a rescue mission for an astronaut on a doomed journey into outer space. Perhaps unsurprisingly, given the scale of his novels, Liu's works have also been adapted for cinema. *The Wandering Earth* had a successful release both in China and internationally in 2019. A film adaptation of *The Three Body Problem* is also in the works.

## Selected Works

NOVELS

*Qiuzhuang Shandian* 球状闪电 (2004). Translated by Jœl Martinsen as *Ball Lightning* (Tor Books, 2018)

*Santi: Diqiu Wangshi* 三体: 地球往事 (2006). Translated by Ken Liu as *The Three-Body Problem* (*The Three Body Problem Series*, 1) (Tor Books, 2014)

*Santi: Heian Senlin* 三体 II: 黑暗森林 (2008). Translated by Jœl Martinsen as *The Dark Forest* (*The Three Body Problem Series*, 2) (Tor Books, 2015)

*Santi: Sishen Yongsheng* 三体 III: 死神永生 (2010). Translated by Ken Liu as *Death's End* (*The Three Body Problem Series*, 3) (Tor Books, 2016)

SHORT STORY COLLECTIONS

*Liulang Diqiu* 流浪地球 (2000). Translated by Holger Nahm as *The Wandering Earth: Classic Science Fiction Collection* (Beijing Qingse Media Company, 2012)

SHORT STORIES

*Rensheng* 人生 (2003). Translated by Ken Liu as 'The Weight of

Memories', published online at https://www.tor.com/2016/08/17/the-weight-of-memories/ (2016)

*Shanyang Shangdi*赡养上帝 (2005). Translated by Ken Liu as 'Taking Care of God' (*Pathlight* Magazine, 2012)

*Yueye*月夜 (2009). Translated by Ken Liu as 'Moonlight' in *Broken Stars* (Tor Books, 2019)

*Huangjin Yuanye* 黄金原野 (2018). Translated by Ken Liu as 'Fields of Gold' in *Twelve Tomorrows* (The MIT Press, 2018)

AC

# LIU HENG
刘恒 (1954–)

Like many writers born in 1950s' China, Liu Heng was a peasant, a worker and a soldier before becoming a writer and playwright. He adopted his own novella *Fuxi Fuxi* (伏羲伏羲) into the movie *Ju Dou* (菊豆) directed by Zhang Yimou.

Liu Heng was born in Beijing and found success early. He published his first collection of short stories, *Small Millstone* (小石磨), in 1977, just a year after the end of the Cultural Revolution. He writes realistic fiction that exposes the dark side of society, but often with humor. His 1999 novel *The Happy Life of Chatterbox Zhang Damin* (贫嘴张大民的幸福生活, not translated) was adapted into a TV mini-series. A self-described introvert, Liu Heng rarely gives interviews. But speaking with the TV journalist He Dong in 2015, he opened up about his views on the use of humor in writing, saying 'Comedy and humor are means and methods of salvation for the human soul.'

## Selected Works

NOVELS

*Hei de Xue* 黑的雪 (1993). Translated by Howard Goldblatt as *Black Snow: A Novel of the Beijing Demimonde* (Grove Press, 1994)

*Cang He Bairimeng* 苍河白日梦 (2009). Translated by Howard Goldblatt as *Green River Daydream* (Grove Press, 2002)

SHORT STORIES

*Gouri de Liangshi* 狗日的粮食 (2003). Translated by Sabrina Knight as 'Dogshit Food', collected in *The Columbia Anthology of Modern Chinese Literature* (Columbia University Press, 2007)

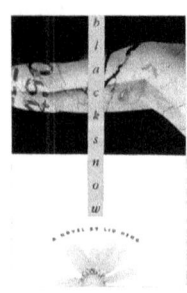

# LIU SUOLA
## 刘索拉 <sup>(1955-)</sup>

Liu Suola was born in Beijing and is an acclaimed musician, composer, and author. She is considered a member of China's Avant-Garde movement which emerged in the 1980s. Despite being born into an elite family, Liu's childhood was affected by the Cultural Revolution, with her parents being sent to the countryside for two decades. Reflections on the Cultural Revolution and its impact recur throughout her work. Liu lived outside China between 1988 and 2002, moving between London and New York, before returning to Beijing. One of her best-known novels, *Chaos and All That: An Irreverent Novel* (混沌加哩咯楞) translated into English by Richard King, was written during her time living in London.

Much of Liu's work captures the experience of Chinese artists in the 1980s and 1990s. Her novella *You Have No Choice* (你别无选择, not translated) encapsulates the mood of artists and intellectuals during the 1980s and was awarded First Prize for Translation by the British Comparative Literature Association. *Chaos and All That* is inflected with Liu's own life experience; the protagonist reflects on her life in China after moving to London, and the novel moves between a first-person confessional narrative and a detached narration in the third person. Alongside her novels, Liu has also written the librettos for a number of her own operas.

## Selected Work

NOVEL

*Hundun Jia Li Ge Leng* 混沌加哩咯楞 (1989). Translated as *Chaos and All That: An Irreverent Novel* by Richard King (University of Hawaii Press, 1994)

AC

# LIU XINWU
## 刘心武 (1942– )

Liu Xinwu was born in Chengdu, Sichuan province. He is considered a member of the older generation of Chinese writers that includes Mo Yan and Jia Pingwa, although they are a decade younger than him. Liu worked as a high school teacher throughout the Cultural Revolution, and it was his short story 'Class Counsellor' (班主任), published in 1977, that established him on the literary scene. The short story is widely considered to be one of the first pieces of literature to denounce the Cultural Revolution. Liu's later work *The Bell and the Drum Tower* (钟鼓楼) won the Mao Dun Literature Prize in 1985. Following the Tiananmen Square protests in 1989, Liu left his position as editor at the state-run People's Literature publishers and turned instead to the study of Cao Xueqin's classic eighteenth-century novel *The Dream of the Red Chamber* (红楼梦).

'Class Coounsellor' is set in a Beijing high school and revolves around events leading up to the fall of the Gang of Four in 1976. The story caused a lot of controversy when it was first published, with readers from across the country writing to *People's Literature* (人民文学) where the story was published. *The Bell and the Drum Tower* is also set in Beijing, taking place in an old-style courtyard complex close to the Gulou area in the centre of the city. The action takes place over the course of twelve hours, centering on one family and the wedding ceremony of their second son. Beyond writing, Liu is a keen painter and an avid football fan.

## Selected Works

NOVEL
*Zhonggulou* 钟鼓楼 (1980). Translated as *The Bell and the Drum Tower* by Jeremy Tiang (New World Press, 1993)

ESSAYS AND REPORTAGE
*Black Walls and Other Stories*, translated by Don Cohn with an introduction by Gérémie Barmé (Renditions, 1990)

SHORT STORY
*Banzhuren* 班主任 (1977). Translated as 'Class Counsellor' by Gérémie Barmé and Bennett Lee, published in *The Wounded: New Stories of the Cultural Revolution* (Joint Publishing, 1979)

AC

# LIU ZHENYUN

刘震云 <sup></sup>(1958– )

Liu Zhenyun was born in Yanjin, Henan province. He is famous for writing novels that capture the realities of urban life in China, and is a commercial success, having sold fifteen million books in China alone. In 2011 he won the prestigious Mao Dun Literature Prize for his work *Someone to Talk To* (一句顶一万句) and in 2018, he received France's Chevalier de l'ordre des Arts et des Lettres. Liu has successfully adapted many of his novels into films in partnership with the director Feng Xiaogang, and writes the screenplays for all the film adaptations of his works.

Liu's breakout work, *Cellphone* (手机), tells the story of a TV presenter whose seemingly perfect life falls apart after he accidentally misplaces his mobile phone. *Someone To Talk To* focuses on the unhappy marriage and tragic family life of a tofu peddler, while *I Did Not Kill My Husband* (我不是潘金莲) is a satire about a woman attempting to get around the restrictions of China's One Child policy. Each work comments on urban modernity, loneliness, and the uncertainty of truth in an authoritarian state.

## Selected Works

NOVELS

*Yi Ju Ding Yi Wan Ju* 一句顶一万句 (2009). Translated as *Someone To Talk To* by Sylvia Li-chun Lin and Howard Goldblatt (Duke University Press, 2018)

*Wo jiao Liu Yuejin* 我叫刘跃进 (2007), translated as *The Cook, the Crook, and the Real Estate Tycoon* by Sylvia Li-chun Lin & Howard Goldblatt (Arcade, 2015)

*Wo Bu Shi Pan Jinlian* 我不是潘金莲 (2012). Translated as *I Did Not Kill My Husband* by Sylvia Li-chun Lin and Howard Goldblatt (Arcade, 2014)

*Shouji* 手机 (2003). Translated as *Cellphone* by Howard Goldblatt (MerwinAsia, 2011)

SHORT STORY COLLECTION

*Wengu Yi Jiu Si Er* 温故一九四二 (2009). Translated as *Remembering 1942: And Other Chinese Stories* by Sylvia Li-chun Lin and Howard Goldblatt (Arcade, 2016)

AC

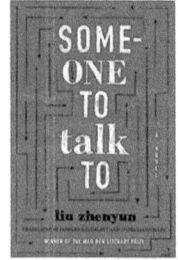

# LU MIN
鲁敏 (1973– )

Lu Min was born in Jiangsu into an educated family (her mother was a teacher and her father an engineer.) She started work as a post office clerk at the age of eighteen and held many other jobs before starting to write at the age of twenty-five. She remembers the famous novelist Su Tong coming in one day to buy stamps and says she felt the spirit of literature in his presence and was so affected that she thought of resigning immediately to go home and write.

Lu Min's best known novels include *Dinner for Six* and *This Love Could Not be Delivered*. She has received numerous awards in China including, in 2009, the highly prestigious Lu Xun Literary Prize. She was also named one of the Top Twenty Future Masters by People's Literature, and Taiwan's *Unitas* magazine's 20 Under 40 top Sinophone writers.

Her short stories, including 'Paradise Temple' (西天寺), 'Hidden Diseases' (暗疾), 'Xie Bomao R.I.P.' (谢伯茂之死), 'A Second Pregnancy 1980' (1980年的第二胎) and 'The Banquet' (大宴), have been translated into English and many are available online. Her 2012 novel *Dinner for Six* (六人晚

餐) has been adapted into a 2017 film Youth Dinner, and an English translation is now in preparation. She lives in Beijing.

## Selected Works

NOVELS

*Liuren Wancan* 六人晚餐 (2012). Translated by Nicky Harman and Helen Wang (Balestier Press, forthcoming, 2022)
*Ci Qing Wu Fa Toudi* 此情无法投递 (2010). Translated by Ian Clark as *This Love Could Not be Delivered* (Simon & Schuster, 2016)

SHORT STORIES

*An Ji* 暗疾 (2011). Translated by Annelise Finegan Wasmœn as 'Hidden Diseases' in *Pathlight: New Chinese Writing* (July 2012)
*Fengyue Jian* 风月剪 (2019). Translated by Michæl Day as 'Scissors, Shining' (*Words without Borders*, June-July 2019)
*Xie Bomao Zhi Si* 谢伯茂之死 (2012). Translated by Helen Wang as 'Xie Bomao RIP' (*Read Paper Republic* October 29, 2015)

ESSAYS

*1980 Nian De Er Tai*, 1980年的二胎 (2015). Translated by Helen Wang as 'A Second Pregnancy 1980' (*Read Paper Republic*, November 3, 2015)

# LU NEI
路内 <sup>(1973– )</sup>

Born in Suzhou, Jiangsu Province, Lu Nei is one of China's best known 'post-70s' writers, yet he only began writing in 2008. At nineteen years old, he was working in menial jobs, drifted, explored, and made many observations of life through his various experiences. (He has had a wide range of jobs, including factory worker, shop assistant, salesperson, warehouse manager, radio announcer, and creative director for an advertising agency.) While working in one factory he had time on his hands and began reading.

Lu Nei has described himself as 'one of the least educated young writers in China.' He has also said he likes to 'write about things that are at the tipping point,' things that are in transition. He writes about what is familiar, his own experiences and observations. His 2007 debut novel, *Young Babylon* (少年巴比伦), has been described as China's *Catcher in the Rye*. It recounts the semi-farcical adventures of a young man much like himself, while his second novel, *The Journeys that Followed Her* (追随她的旅程, not translated), is the story of a group of disaffected youths in a small town who suddenly decide to take their futures into their own hands.

Lu, who now lives in Shanghai, is also the fiction moderator for the so-called 'underliterature' section of the Chinese-language independent literary website, sickbaby. org. Asked which of his works he would most want to be read outside China, Lu suggested *Young Babylon* and *Compassion* (慈悲). He is quoted as saying that '*Compassion...* is a story spanning almost fifty years, and offers some new insights on China, [politically] a bit on the left and a bit on the right. Also, I want to discuss in the novel whether Chinese people have a sense of religious faith. The Chinese are often thought of as atheists, but there are actually a large number of Christians and Buddhists. Buddhism has a lot of secular elements, and in that sense, whether that can constitute a sense of spirituality in the Chinese people and whether that can make them happy and lead them to do good – that is what I want to discuss in the novel. *Young Babylon* is different. There are many politically incorrect things in the novel, and I want to see how foreign readers respond to that.'

## Selected Works

NOVELS

*Shaonian Babilun* 少年巴比伦 (2008). Translated by Poppy Toland as *Young Babylon* (Amazon Crossing, 2015)

*Huajie Wangshi* 花街往事 (2014). Translated by Poppy Toland as *A Tree Grows in Daicheng* (Amazon Crossing, 2017)

*Cibei* 慈悲 (2016). Translated by Nicky Harman for the Chinese publishers, as *Compassion*. Publication status unknown.

SHORT STORY COLLECTION

*Shiqi Sui de Qing Qibing* 十七岁的轻骑兵 (2012). Translated by Zhu

Jinwen, Anna Holmwood, Chris Burrow, and Rachel Henson as *The 17-Year-Old Hussars* (Shanghai Press, 2016).

SHORT STORIES

*Ah-Di, Ni Manman Pao* 阿弟，你慢慢跑. Translated by Rachel Henson as 'Keep Running, Little Brother' in *Read Paper Republic* (2015).

*Yaoguai de Paiqiu* 妖怪打排球 (2012). Translated by Anna Holmwood as 'Monster at Volleyball' in *Chutzpah!* (2015)

*Zai Wuding Shang Mu Yun* 在屋顶上牧云. Translated by Ed Allen as 'Herding Clouds on the Rooftop' in *Literary Shanghai* (2020)

FB

# LU XUN
鲁迅<sup>(1881–1936)</sup>

Lu Xun (a.k.a. Lu Hsün, pen name of Zhou Shuren 周
树人, 1881–1936) was the preeminent Chinese writer of
the early twentieth century. Born into a declining family
of landlords and scholar officials in Shaoxing, Zhejiang
Province, Lu Xun initially trained as a medical doctor in
Japan from 1902–1906, but abandoned his studies to turn to
writing. This change in direction was purportedly triggered
when he saw a photograph of a Chinese man about to be
beheaded by the Japanese military. Lu Xun's anger was
directed less at the executioners than at the apparent apathy
and callousness of the Chinese onlookers, and he set about
using his literary skills to change Chinese culture.

During his lifetime, he produced essays, translations,
poems and short stories, the best-known of which are *A
Madman's Diary* (1918), *Kong Yiji* (1919) and *The True Story
of Ah Q* (1921). Lu Xun is closely associated with the May
Fourth Movement of 1919—an anti-imperialist cultural
movement that grew out of student protests against China's
humiliation at the Treaty of Versailles at the conclusion of
the First World War—thus was primarily a leftist, and was

much admired by Mao Zedong, though he never joined the Communist Party, and had many conflicts with early Communist figures. He remains hugely influential in China, where his writings are part of the middle school curriculum, and are still studied and discussed by contemporary authors.

For a full account of Lu Xun's life and influence, see Julia Lovell's excellent introduction to Lu Xun's life and writing in *The Real Story of Ah-Q and Other Tales of China: The Complete Fiction of Lu Xun*, (Penguin Classics, 2009). Lovell concludes as follows: 'Lu Xun's life, work and afterlife are a testament to the creativity, cosmopolitanism and intellectual independence of twentieth-century Chinese culture, and to the uncertainties and constraints imposed upon it. Though too often he allowed his own creativity to be derailed by an uncertain temper and provincial infighting, though he subjected his own responses and actions to an almost paralysing self-scrutiny that prevented him from moving beyond short fiction to the novel, he at least succeeded in never falling silent – reading, thinking and writing through exceptional political, social and personal upheaval. For his tonal control, his restless experimentalism and his passionate seriousness of purpose, Lu Xun deserves his accolades, and still has much to teach his contemporary counterparts.'

## Selected Works

SHORT STORY AND ESSAY COLLECTIONS

*Jottings under Lamplight*, essays by Lu Xun, various translators, edited by Eileen Cheng and Kirk Denton, (Harvard University Press, 2017)
*The Real Story of Ah-Q and Other Tales of China: The Complete Fiction of*

*Lu Xun*, translated by Julia Lovell (Penguin Classics, 2009)
*Silent China: Selected Writings of Lu Xun*, translated by Gladys Yang (Oxford University Press,1973)
*Selected Stories of Lu Hsün* translated by Yang Hsien-yi and Gladys Yang, (Foreign Languages Press, 1960)

POETRY COLLECTIONS
*Ye Cao* (野草), prose poems, translated by Matt Turner as *Weeds* (Seaweed Salad, 2019)
*Lu Xun: Selected Poems*, translated by WJF Jenner (University Press of the Pacific, 2001)

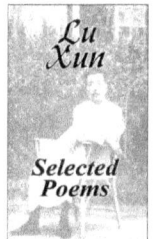

# MA JIAN
馬建 <sup>(1953–)</sup>

Born in Qingdao, Shandong Province, Ma Jian is an
internationally reknowned Chinese writer and artist, who
lives in London in semi-exile. He is a vocal critic of the
Chinese government and has been denied entry to the
mainland since 2011. Most of his books are not available in
China.

Ma Jian grew up during turbulent times. His school
education was cut short by the Cultural Revolution, and
he taught himself to write by copying a Chinese dictionary
one word at a time. His education included time spent
with a painter persecuted for being a 'rightist'. He joined
a propaganda arts troupe and worked as a watch-mender's
apprentice. He also worked in a petrochemical factory. In
1979, he moved to Beijing and became a photojournalist
for the All-China Federation of Trade Unions. During the
Beijing years, he was part of the underground No Name
art group, the Yuanmingyuan poetry group, and the April
photographers' group. He held clandestine exhibitions in a
room in Nanxiao Lane, which became a meeting point for
dissident artists and writers in Beijing.

During the Anti-Spiritual Pollution Campaign in China in 1983, his paintings were denounced and he was placed in detention. After his release, he resigned from his job and set off on a three-year journey through China, selling his paintings and stories as he went. When he returned to Beijing in 1986, he wrote *Stick Out Your Tongue* (亮出你的舌苔或空空荡荡), a novella inspired by his travels through Tibet. Its publication in the official journal *People's Literature* in February 1987 coincided with a nationwide crackdown on the arts, and the government publicly denounced the work as an example of bourgeois liberalism. All copies of the journal were confiscated and destroyed, and a blanket ban was placed on future publication of Ma Jian's books.

In 1986, Ma Jian moved to Hong Kong, but in 1989 he returned to Beijing and took part in the pro-democracy protests. After the June Fourth protest movement, he remained in the capital and wrote *The Noodle Maker* (拉面者), a dark political satire. After the 1997 handover of Hong Kong, he left China for good, moving first to Germany then to London where he now resides. In Germany and London, he worked on *Beijing Coma* (肉之土), a novel about the June Fourth movement and the decade of political repression and economic growth that followed it.

*Red Dust* (红尘), a fictionalised account of his journey through China in the 1980s, won the 2002 Thomas Cook Travel Book Award.

# Selected Works

NOVELS

*Zhongguo Meng* 中国梦 (2018). Translated by Flora Drew as *China Dream* (Counterpoint, 2020)

*Yin zhi Dao* 阴之道 (2013). Translated by Flora Drew as *The Dark Road* (Penguin Books, 2014)

*Rou zhi Tu* 肉之土 (2008). Translated by Flora Drew as *Beijing Coma* (Vintage Books USA, 2009)

*Lamianzhe* 拉面者 (1991). Translated by Flora Drew as *The Noodle Maker* (Picador, 2006)

*Liangchu Nide Shetai huo Kongkongdangdang* 亮出你的舌苔或空空荡荡 (1987). Translated by Flora Drew as *Stick Out Your Tongue* (Picador, 2007)

NON-FICTION

*Hong Chen* 红尘 (2002). Translated by Flora Drew as *Red Dust: A Path Through China* (Anchor, 2002)

FB

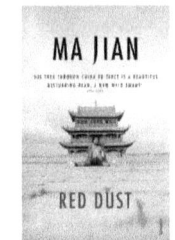

# MAI JIA
麦家 <sup>(1964– )</sup>

Mai Jia is the pen name of Jian Benhu. He was born in Fuyang, Zhejiang province in 1964 and writes historical fiction with a focus on espionage and code breaking. He is one of China's most commercially successful authors. In his early adulthood, Mai Jia spent seventeen years in the People's Liberation Army; his involvement in intelligence training provides inspiration for much of his work. Mai Jia has published three novels to date, all of which are bestsellers in China. In 2007, when his novel *The Message* (风声) was published, Mai became the highest paid author in China at the time. This commercial success has translated into adaptations for both the big and small screens. In 2009, Taiwanese director Chen Kuofu (陈国富) adopted *The Message* for film. Since then, Mai has written a screenplay for a TV series that acts as the novel's sequel. He is also working on turning this screenplay into three further full-length novels. Mai Jia has also received critical recognition, most notably winning China's top literary prize, the Mao Dun Prize, in 2008.

Mai Jia's three novels are set during the Republican

Period (1912–1949) and feature characters who are incredibly clever, but burdened by emotional or psychological flaws. His debut, *Decoded* (解密), features a renowned codebreaker, whilst *In the Dark* (暗算) looks at China's secret service 'Unit 701.' *The Message* tells the story of a group of counterinsurgency officers working in Hangzhou during the Japanese Occupation. Despite his significant success, Mai does not chase the limelight. He lives in Hangzhou and, from time to time, will entirely cut himself off from the world in order to write.

## Selected Works

NOVELS

*Fengsheng* 风声 (2007). Translated by Olivia Milburn as *The Message* (Head of Zeus, 2020)

*Ansuan* 暗算 (2003). Translated by Olivia Milburn as *In the Dark* (Penguin, 2015)

*Jiemi* 解密 (2002). Translated by Olivia Milburn and Christopher Payne as *Decoded* (Farrar, Strauss and Giroux, 2014)

AC

# MIAN MIAN

## 棉棉 <sup>(1970– )</sup>

Mian Mian writes about her native Shanghai. In her works she depicts its underground music scene and addresses once-taboo topics such as promiscuous sex, drugs, and suicide. *Candy* (糖) is semi-autobiographical, weaving together stories from when she was a heroin addict. Although banned in China – and despite Mian Mian's label as the 'poster child for spiritual pollution' – the original still sold well. One of her novels, *Shanghai Panic* (我们害怕, not translated), was even made into a film in which she played a leading role.

## Selected Works

**NOVELS**

*Shizong Biaoyan* 失踪表演. Translated by Andrea Lingenfelter as *Vanishing Act* (Editions Sébastien Moreu, 2019)

*Tang* 糖 (China Theatre Press, 2000) Translated by Andrea Lingenfelter as *Candy* (Back Bay Books, 2003)

REC

# MO YAN
莫言 <sup>(1955-)</sup>

Mo Yan was born in Gaomi County, Shandong province.
He is one of China's most celebrated living writers and was a
leading figure in the 'roots seeking movement' (寻根运动) of
the 1980s. (This movement was largely made up of writers
who sought to capture China's rural and minority cultures
in their fiction.) In 2012, Mo Yan won the Nobel Prize for
Literature, becoming the first Chinese national living in
China to receive the accolade, and he is one of the most
widely translated of Chinese writers. His breakout work *Red
Sorghum* (红高粱家族, 1986) was adapted into a film in 1987,
directed by Zhang Yimou.

Mo Yan's works are often set in Shandong villages, not
dissimilar to his hometown. *Red Sorghum* chronicles the
life of a rural Shandong family from the Sino-Japanese war
to Mao's death in 1976. He has cited William Faulkner
and Gabriel García Márquez as influences on his work,
and his novel *Republic of Wine* (酒国), the story of a cadre
sent to investigate accusations of cannibalism in a far-away
province, offers Mo Yan's own take on 'magical realism.' Mo
Yan is sometimes regarded overseas as 'pro-government',

and yet he hasn't shied away from political themes: *The Garlic Ballads* (天堂蒜薹的歌), published in 1988, uses the 1987 garlic surplus to comment on local government, whilst his 2009 novel *Frog* (蛙) reflects on the consequences of the One Child Policy. Aside from his novels, Mo Yan has also published a number of novellas, short stories, and one play.

## Selected Works

NOVELS

*Wa* 蛙 (2009), translated as *Frog* by Howard Goldblatt (Viking, 2015)

*Tanxiang Xing* 檀香刑 (2001), translated by Howard Goldblatt as *Sandalwood Death* (University of Oklahoma Press, 2012)

*Sishiyi Pao* 四十一炮 (2003), translated by Howard Goldblatt as *Pow!* (University of Chicago Press, 2012)

*Sheng Si Pilao* 生死疲劳 (2006), translated by Howard Goldblatt as *Life and Death Are Wearing Me Out* (Arcade, 2008)

*Feng Ru Fei Tun* 丰乳肥臀 (1995), translated by Howard Goldblatt as *Big Breasts & Wide Hips* (Arcade Publishing, 2004)

*Jiu Guo* 酒國 (1998), translated by Howard Goldblatt as *The Republic of Wine: A Novel* (Arcade Publishing, 2000)

*Tiantang Suantai Zhi Ge* 天堂蒜薹的歌 (1988), translated by Howard Goldblatt as *The Garlic Ballads: A Novel* (Viking, 1995)

*Hong Gaoliang Jiazu* 紅高粱家族 (1986), translated by Howard Goldblatt as *Red Sorghum: A Novel of China* (Viking Penguin, 1993)

SHORT STORY COLLECTIONS

*Shifu Yuelai Yue Youmo* 师傅越来越幽默 (2000) translated by Howard Goldblatt as *Shifu, You'll Do Anything for a Laugh* (Arcade Publishing, 2001)

*Explosions and Other Stories* (ed. Janice Wickeri), translated by Janice Wickeri and Duncan Hewitt (Renditions Books, Chinese University of Hong Kong, 1991)

# MURONG XUEXUN
# 慕容雪村<sup>(1974–)</sup>

Murong Xuecun is the pen name of the Chinese novelist Hao Qun (郝群), one of China's first Internet-based writers. His 2003 debut work *Leave Me Alone: A Novel of Chengdu* (成都, 今夜请将我遗忘) propelled him to stardom. His 2008 novel *Dancing through Red Dust* (原谅我红尘颠倒) was longlisted for the Man Asian Literary Prize and was later adapted into a TV series.

Murong's darkly funny writing deals mostly with social issues in contemporary China such as corruption, business-government relations, and general disillusionment with modern life. His literature is known for its nihilistic, realist, and fatalist style. In 2009, Murong wrote, 'China: In the Absence of a Remedy' (中国，少了一味药, not translated), an exposé of a pyramid scheme in Jiangxi province that he had become entangled in. This earned him the 2010 People's Literature Prize; in his acceptance speech, he lambasted his editor and the Chinese state in general, and recently has been unable to publish his work in China (although his older books are still available). He has also written op-eds for *The New York Times*.

# Selected Works

**NOVELS**

*Yuanliang Wo Hongchen Diandao* 原谅我红尘颠倒. Translated by Harvey Thomlinson as *Dancing through Red Dust* (Fortysix, 2015)
*Chengdu, Jinye Qing Jiang Wo Yiwang* 成都，今夜请将我遗忘. Translated by Harvey Thomlinson as *Leave Me Alone: A Novel of Chengdu* (Make-Do Publishing, 2009)

**SHORT STORIES**

*Shigu* 事故. Translated by Harvey Thomlinson as 'The Accident' (*The Guardian*, 2012)

**ESSAYS**

*No Roads Are Straight Here*. Translated by Jane Weizhen Pan and Martin Merz (*NY Times*, 2012)
*Absurdities of China's Censorship System*. Translated by Harvey Thomlinson, Jane Weizhen Pan and Martin Merz (*Time* magazine, 2011)
*Words We Can Use, and Those We Cannot*. Translated by Harvey Thomlinson, Jane Weizhen Pan and Martin Merz (*NY Times*, 2011)
*Dreaming of a Normal Life in China*. Translated by Jane Weizhen Pan and Martin Merz (*NY Times*, 2011)
*Caging a Monster*. Translated by Jane Weizhen Pan and Martin Merz (*China Heritage Quarterly*, 2011)

AG

# PRIEST
## Priest <sup>(1988– )</sup>

Priest, or 'p大', known in fandom as 'pipi' (皮皮) and 'sweet' (甜甜), is one of China's best-known and highly acclaimed online literary authors. A graduate of Shanghai Jiao Tong University, she also holds a Master's degree from Hong Kong University of Science and Technology. She published her first novel in 2007. Priest writes in a wide range of genres, including *danmei* (耽美), or 'indulging beauty.' *Danmei* novels are typically written by female writers for female audiences; the theme is male-male romance – however, the gaze is female rather than male.

Many of Priest's online novels have also been published in print; even more have been adapted into TV dramas. Her works have won multiple awards in different genres ranging from science fiction to mystery.

## Selected Works

NOVELS

*You Fei*有匪 (2015). Translated as Bandits with multiple online translations (non-official) on sites such as mtlnovel.com and elentiyalæ.

com; a TV adaptation was entitled *Legend of Fei*.

*Zhen Hun* 镇魂 (2012). Translated as *Guardian* (novel) online at mtlnovel.com

*Shan He Biao Li* 山河表里 (2014). Translated as *Guardians of the Lands* (novel) online at mtlnovel.com

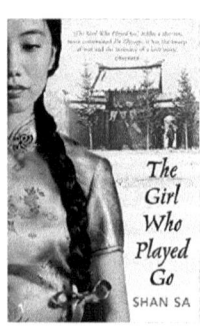

# SHAN SA

山飒 <sup>(1972–)</sup>

山飒 (1972–)

Shan Sa is the pen name of Chinese-French novelist, poet, and painter Yan Ni (阎妮). After finishing secondary school in her hometown Beijing, she moved to Paris with her father who taught at the Sorbonne. In 2001, she published the highly acclaimed *La Joueuse de Go (The Girl Who Played Go)* in French; this has now been translated into thirty-two languages. Focusing on a young Go master in Manchuria, the novel uses the strategy game as a metaphor for the Japanese invasion. It won the Prix Goncourt des Lycéens award in 2001 and the 2004 Kiriyama Prize for fiction.

Shan Sa's 2003 biographical novel *Impératrice (Empress)* is based on the legendary Chinese empress Wu Zetian. Her other prize-winning novels, such as 1999's *Les Quatre Vies du Saule (The Four Lives of the Willow)* are also published in French. Shan Sa writes poetry in Chinese and French and exhibits her paintings internationally. She currently lives in Paris.

# Selected Works

NOVELS

*La Joueuse de Go*. Translated from the French by Adriana Hunter as *The Girl Who Played Go* (Vintage, 2003)

# SHENG KEYI
盛可以 [(1973– )]

Born in an isolated village in Hunan Province, Sheng
Keyi lived for a time in Shenzhen before moving to Beijing.
She worked a host of different jobs, including secretary,
reporter and editor, before giving them all up to focus on
writing. Sheng is of the generation of writers who deal
primarily with urban China, as opposed to rural themes, and
focuses in particular on the survival of the poor in big cities.
She is experimental with style and voice and her works
cover a wide spectrum of emotional and social territory.
She has been awarded many prizes, including the Chinese
People's Literature Prize, the Yu Dafu Prize for Fiction, the
Chinese Literature Media Award and the Top 20 Novelists
of the Future Prize. Shelly Bryant's translation of her work
*Northern Girls* (北妹) was shortlisted for the Man Asian
Literary Prize.

In an interview with *Griffith Review*, Sheng said, 'My
interest is in creative fiction; that is my art. [Fiction] has a
bigger scope for imagination [than journalistic writing] and
there is a bigger scope for participation in a fictionalised
space. By writing fiction I can be embodied in a character

and have a different experience, or I can look into the future and see really far. It has a greater capacity for exploring the possibilities of the world.'

## Selected Works

NOVELS

*Yeman Shengzhang* 野蛮生长 (2015). Translated by Shelly Bryant as *Wild Fruit* (Viking/Penguin, 2019)

*Siwang Fuge* 死亡赋格 (2013). Translated by Shelly Bryant as *Death Fugue* (Giramondo Books, 2014)

*Bei Mei* 北妹 (2004). Translated by Shelly Bryant as *Northern Girls* (Penguin Books, 2012)

*Bai Caodi* 白草地 (2010). Translated by Shelly Bryant as *Fields of White* (Penguin Books, 2014)

SHORT STORIES

*Meiyou chuiyan de cunzhuang* 没有炊烟的村庄 (2012). Translated by Brendan O'Kane as 'A Village of Cold Hearths' (*Chinese Literature Today*, 2015)

*Yu Ci* 鱼刺 (2002). Translated by Shelly Bryant as 'Fishbone' (*Pathlight*, 2012)

*Quefa Jingyan de Shijie* 缺乏经验的世界. Translated by Eric Abrahamsen as 'An Inexperienced World' (2009)

*Mai shouji de guniang* 卖手机的姑娘. Translated by Brendan O'Kane as 'The Girl Who Sold Phones' (*Chinese Literature Today*, 2011)

*Xi Hong Yi* 惜红衣, translated by John Barthlette as 'Little Girl Lost' (*Words Without Borders*, 2008)

REC

# SHUANG XUETAO

双雪涛<sup>(1982– )</sup>

Shang Xuetao is a novelist from the city of Shenyang, and a member of the 'New Northeast Writers Group' (新东北作家群). He gave up an office job in a bank order to pursue writing. His first novel, *A Ghost with Wings* (翅鬼, untranslated) was published in 2011, and won the first Chinese World Literature Award for Film in Taiwan. He also won the Taipei Literature Award and New Voices Award. His other published works include *Moses on the Plain* (平原上的摩西, currently being translated), and *The Aviator* (飞行家, untranslated). Some of his books have been adapted into films.

In 2020 Shuang won the Blancpain-Imaginist Literary Prize (宝珀理想国文学奖) for his work *The Hunter* (猎人, untranslated). Speaking on behalf of the judges as Shuang was awarded the 30,000 RMB prize, the writer Su Tong remarked: 'We have seen what the author has achieved in his writing and the quality of his creations. … We share a sense of wonder at the author's spiritual adventures. We thank the author for creating a new electrifying literary field for us, for giving us another whirling dizziness.'

## Selected Works

SHORT STORIES

*Qiaoqiaoban*跷跷板. Translated by Jeremy Tiang as 'Teeter-Totter' in *Brick* (2019)

*Dashi*大师. Translated by Michæl Day as 'The Master' in *Pathlight* (Winter, 2015)

FB

# SU TONG

苏童 (1963–)

Su Tong (the penname of Tong Zhonggui) rose to international fame in 1993 following the release of Zhang Yimou's Oscar-nominated film, *Raise the Red Lantern*, which was based on his novella *Wives and Concubines* (妻妾成群). He has had a number of works translated into English, including *Madwoman on the Bridge* (桥上的疯妈妈), Check, a violent drama set in the aftermath of the Cultural Revolution, and most recently, *Shadow of the Hunter* (黄雀记). He received the Man Asian Literary Prize in 2009 for *The Boat to Redemption* (河岸) and was a finalist for the Man Booker International Prize in 2011. He was born in Suzhou, from which he adapted his pen name, meaning 'child of Suzhou', and now lives in Beijing with his family.

## Selected Works

NOVELS

*Huang Que Ji* 黄雀记 (2013). Translated by James Trapp as *Shadow of the Hunter* (Sinoist Books, 2020)

*He'an* 河岸 (2009). Translated by Howard Goldblatt as *Boat to Redemption* (Black Swan, 2016)

*Cheng Bei Didai* 城北地带 (2004). Translated by Howard Goldblatt as *Binu and the Great Wall* (Canongate U.S., 2008)

*Wo de Diwang Shengya* 我的帝王生涯 (1992). Translated by Howard Goldblatt as *My Life As Emperor* (Hyperion, 2006)

*Mi* 米 (1991). Translated by Howard Goldblatt as *Rice* (Harper Perennial, 2004)

*Qiqie Cheng Qun* 妻妾成群 (1991). Translated by Michæl Duke as *Raise the Red Lantern* (W. Morrow and Company, 1993)

*Hongfen* 红分 (2004). Translated by Martin Merz and Jane Weizhen Pan as *Petulia's Rouge Tin* (Penguin Specials, 2018)

*San Zhan Deng* 三盏灯 (2010). Translated by Kyle Anderson as *Three-Lamp Lantern* (Simon and Schuster, 2016)

*Ling Yizhong Funü Shenghuo* 另一种妇女生活 (2003). Translated by Kyle Anderson as *Another Life for Women* (Simon & Schuster, 2016)

SHORT STORY COLLECTIONS

*Qiaoshang de Fengmama* 桥上的疯妈妈 (2005). Translated by Josh Stenberg as *Madwoman on the Bridge* (Black Swan, 2008)

REC

222

# TANG FEI
糖匪 [(1983– )]

Tang Fei is the pen-name of the prolific Chinese science fiction writer Wang Jing (王璟). A graduate of Shanghai Jiao Tong University, she mainly writes speculative novellas and short stories. Her fiction has been featured in magazines in China, such as *Science Fiction World*, and shortlisted for various Best Science Fiction of the Year awards. Her stories have been translated into English and published in the United Kingdom and the United States. Her major works include 'Call Girls' (*Huangse gushi*黄色故事), which was reprinted in Rich Horton's The Year's Best Science Fiction & Fantasy 2014, and 'Broken Stars'(*Sui xingxing* 碎星星).

## Selected Works

SHORT STORIES

*Sui Xingxing* 碎星星. Translated by Ken Liu as 'Broken Stars', collected in *Broken Stars: Contemporary Chinese Science Fiction in Translation* (Tor Books, 2020)

*Xiongmao Siyangyuan* 熊貓飼養員. Translated by Tony Huang as 'Panda Breeder' in *SmokeLong Quarterly* (September 2019)

*Wu Ding Xixing Ji* 无定西行记. Translated by Andy Dudak as 'Wu Ding's Journey to the West' in *Clarkesworld* 154 (July, 2019)

*Kanjian Jingyuzuo de Ren* 看见鲸鱼座的人. Translated by S. Qiouyi Lu as 'The Person Who Saw Cetus' in *Clarkesworld* 128 (May, 2017)

*Ziyou Zhilu* 自由之路. Translated by Christine Ni as 'The Path to Freedom', *Read Paper Republic* (December, 2016)

*Yuzhou Aige* 宇宙哀歌. Translated by John Chu as 'A Universal Elegy' in *Clarkesworld* 100 (January, 2015)

*Pupu* 蒲蒲. Translated by John Chu as 'Pepe' in *Clarkesworld* 93 (June, 2014).

*Huangse Gushi* 黄色故事. Translated by Ken Liu as 'Call Girl' in *APEX Magazine* (June, 2013)

# TIE NING

铁凝 (1957– )

Tie Ning has published more than fifty novels and collections of essays over a long and fruitful literary career. Her major novels include *Meimei Had Never Seen the Mountains* (玫瑰门, lit. *The Rose Gate*), *The Bathing Women* (大浴女) and *Thickheaded Flower* (笨花). She has also written over a hundred novellas and short stories. She has won six national literary prizes, including the Lu Xun Literature Award, and received more than thirty honors for her novels and essays.

The movie *Oh, Xiangxue!*, adapted by Tie Ning from her short story of the same name, was honored at the 41st Berlin International Film Festival, and at China's Golden Rooster and Hundred Flowers film awards. Her work has been translated into many languages. She has been the president of the Chinese Writers Association since 2006. Tie Ning was born in Beijing in 1957 and currently lives in Hebei Province.

## Selected Works

NOVELS

*Dayunü* 大浴女 (2000). Translated by Zhang Honglin and Jason Sommer as *The Bathing Women* (Simon & Schuster US, Harper Collins UK, 2012)

REC

# WANG ANYI
# 王安忆 <sup>(1954-)</sup>

One of China's most famous writers, Wang Anyi frequently sets her stories in her native Shanghai, as well as rural Anhui where she was sent for 're-education' during the Cultural Revolution. She began publishing stories in 1976 and immersed herself in writing when she was allowed to return to Shanghai in 1978. Several of Wang's novellas and stories – notably *Love on a Barren Mountain*, *Love in A Small Town* and *Brocade Valley* (荒山之恋，小城之恋，锦绣谷之恋, known collectively as the *Three Loves* 三恋) – touched upon love and female sexuality in Cultural Revolution and the early reform era, topics still considered to be taboo in the 1980s. Though her style was impressionistic and poetic rather than explicit, her work was nevertheless seen as controversial at the time.

*The Song of Everlasting Sorrow* 长恨歌 (1995) is widely considered to be Wang Anyi's greatest work. The winner of the Mao Dun Prize in 2000, it is an epic, tragic saga, tracing the life and loves of a Shanghai starlet of the 1940s through civil war, to the Cultural Revolution and into the reform era. Critics have seen it as capturing the spirit of Shanghai life in a way rarely seen since the works of Zhang Ailing (Eileen Chang) in the 1940s; it has been adapted for stage, television and cinema.

Wang Anyi won the Newman Prize for Chinese Literature in 2017 and was a finalist for the Man Booker International Prize in 2011. In 2013, she was made a Chevalier de l'Ordre des Arts et des Lettres by the French government. In addition to being widely translated, she has herself translated Elizabeth Swados's picture book, *My Depression: A Picture Book from English*. Since 2006, Wang has been one of the vice-chairs of the China Writers Association; she is also a professor of Chinese literature at Shanghai's Fudan University.

## Selected Works

**NOVELS**

*Fu Ping* 富萍 (2000). Translated by Howard Goldblatt as *Fu Ping* (Columbia University Press, 2019)

*Changhenge* 长恨歌 (1995). Translated by Michæl Berry and Susan Chan Egan as *The Song of Everlasting Sorrow* (Columbia University Press, 2008)

*Xiao Baozhuang* 小鲍庄. Translated by Martha Avery as *Baotown* (Viking, 1988)

**NOVELLAS**

*Jinxiu Gu zhi Lian* 锦绣谷之恋 (1987). Translated by Chen Maiping and Bonnie S. McDougall as *Brocade Valley* (New Directions, 1992) [DH6]

*Huangshan zhi Lian* 荒山之恋 (1986). Translated by Eva Hung as *Love on a Barren Mountain* (Renditions Paperbacks, Chinese University of Hong Kong, 1991)

*Xiao Cheng zhi Lian* 小城之恋 (1986). Translated by Eva Hung as *Love in a Small Town* (Renditions Paperbacks, 1988)

SHORT STORIES

*Afang de Deng* 阿芳的灯 (1986). Translated by Helen Wang as 'Ah Fang's Lamp' (in The Book of Shanghai, Comma Press, 2020)
*Hei Nongtang* 黑弄堂 (2005). Translated by Canaan Morse as 'The Dark Alley' (Read Paper Republic, 2016)

ESSAYS

*Liu Yan* 流言. Translated by Andrew F. Jones as 'Written on Water' (*New York Review of Book*, 2021)
*Duizhaoji* 對照記. Translated by Janice Wickeri as 'Reflections: Words and Pictures' (Excerpts) in *Renditions*, (Chinese University of Hong Kong), Spring 1996
*Si Yu* 私語. Translated by Janet Ng as 'Intimate Words', in *Renditions*, Spring 1996
*Jin Yu Lu* 燼餘錄. Translated by Oliver Stunt as 'From the Ashes', in *Renditions*, Spring 1996

# WANG MENG
王蒙 (1934– )

Wang Meng's story is unusual among Chinese writers. Born in 1934 in Beijing, he began life under Japanese occupation before becoming an ardent supporter of the Communist Party and the Chinese revolutionary cause. His short story 'A Young Man Comes to the Organizational Department', published in 1956, nearly ended Wang's literary career before it had begun: the story's critique of bureaucracy was interpreted as an attack on Party authority. It wasn't until the story came to the attention of Chairman Mao himself, who praised its rebellious spirit, that Wang was assured of a lasting career and reputation.

He and his family eventually spent sixteen years living and working in Yining, near the border with Kazakhstan, during which time he learned the Uighur language and became familiar with local culture. The experience left a profound mark on him as a person and as a writer, and much of his most important later writings draw on his experiences in Xinjiang – most notably the short story 'A Pair of Grey Eyes' and the novel *The Scenery Around Here*. It also confirmed for him the importance of fiction grounded in real experience and real people. Though his literary voice bursts with lyrical creativity, his stories grow from close observation of life.

A year after the end of the Cultural Revolution, Wang and his family returned to Beijing, where he was finally welcomed into literary society. As enthusiasm for culture and literature grew during the 1980s, Wang's cachet continued to rise. He was gradually promoted through the ranks of the Chinese Writers Association and became Minister of Culture in 1986. He lasted three years in office before being dismissed in September 1989 following the crackdown on the Tiananmen protests. The same year also saw the publication of his seminal short story, 'The Stubborn Porridge', an allegorical commentary on reforms.

## Selected Works

NOVEL

*Bu Li* 布礼 (1979). Translated by Wendy Larson as *Bolshevik Salute: A Modernist Chinese Novel* (University of Washington Press, 1989)

SHORT STORY COLLECTIONS

*Jianying de Xizhou* 坚硬的稀粥 (1989). Translated by Zhu Hong as *The Stubborn Porridge* (*The Paris Review*, 1993; also in *Stubborn Porridge and other stories*, George Braziller, 1994)

*Xueqiu Ji* 雪球集 (1989). Translated by Deirdre Huang and Cathy Silber as *Snowball* (Foreign Languages Press, 1989)

*The Butterfly and Other Stories*, translator unknown (Chinese Literature/Panda Books, 1983)

# WANG SHUO

王朔 <sup>(1958– )</sup>

The enfant terrible of Chinese literature in the 1980s and
90s, Wang Shuo was born in Nanjing to a military family of
Manchu origin, but grew up in Beijing. During the Cultural
Revolution, his parents were sent down to the countryside,
leaving Wang and his brother behind to run wild in the city,
a period that formed the backdrop to Wang's 1991 story
'Wild Beasts' (动物凶猛), later adapted into Jiang Wen's film
*In the Heat of the Sun* (1994).

Wang Shuo burst onto the Chinese literary scene in
the mid 1980s, becoming the prime exponent of what was
known to its conservative critics as 'hooligan literature'
(痞子文学), and one of the first Chinese writers to succeed
in commercializing his work. His stories, set in the fast-
changing urban environment of China's 1980s' economic
reforms, often highlighted the darker side of society and
the gap between a more irreverent young generation and its
traditional Communist elders.

Such stories were denounced by party critics as
reactionary and dissolute – but the Sinologist Gérémie

Barmé describes his heroes as 'the modern-day bastard progeny of the knight-errant, urban tricksters armed with a caustic wit which they use to lunge and parry as they make their way in a mendacious world.'

Wang also made a foray into the realm of detective fiction (though he later described this as a mistake), with novels such as *Playing for Thrills* (玩儿的就是心跳, 1989), which had an intriguing central character and an evocative Beijing milieu, but a plot that left many readers scratching their heads. After the crushing of the 1989 protests, Wang Shuo's writing came in for fresh criticism. Yet one of his most satirical novels, *Please Don't Call me Human* (千万别把我当人) appeared in *Harvest* (收获) literary magazine in September 1989. An absurdist and often grotesque satire on Chinese politics and national pride, it revolves around an international sports competition in which China's representative is a Beijing pedicab driver who has learned martial arts skills from his father, the last survivor of the Boxer movement of 1900.

And in the early 1990s, the ever adaptable Wang reinvented himself as a TV screenwriter, resulting in what was known as the 'Wang Shuo phenomenon': 1990's *Yearnings* (渴望) was followed by 1992's *The Story of the Editorial Department* (编辑部的故事), co-written with the film director Feng Xiaogang. This witty satire of life in a magazine office gripped audiences, and provided rare light relief to a nation still reeling from the events of 1989. These were followed by film adaptations including Feng Xiaogang's *Father* and Zhang Yuan's *Little Red Flowers*. After years focusing on TV and movie scripts, Wang returned in 2007 with *My Millennium Chill* (我的千岁寒), a collection of essays, a film script and a short story, and the novel *A Conversation with our Daughter* (和我们的女儿谈话, 2008).

Relatively few of Wang Shuo's works have been fully translated, and the author has not always accepted offers to translate them. Yet despite his stop-start writing career and frequent changes of creative direction, he remains a significant figure on the contemporary Chinese literary scene, never afraid to express his opinions of other authors. A new 15-volume set of Wang Shuo's works was published in China in 2021.

## Selected Works

NOVELS:

*Qianwan Bie Ba Wo Dang Ren* 千万别把我当人 (1989). Translated by Howard Goldblatt as *Please Don't Call Me Human* (Hyperion, 2000)
*Wanr de Jiushi Xintiao* 玩儿的就是心跳 (1989). Translated by Howard Goldblatt as *Playing for Thrills* (Penguin Books, 1998)
*Yiban shi Haishui, Yiban shi Huoyan* 一半是海水，一半是火焰 (1986); excerpt translated by Gérémie Barmé and Linda Jaivin as *Hot and Cold, Measure for Measure*, in Barmé and Jaivin (eds), *New Ghosts, Old Dreams: Chinese Rebel Voices* (Times Books, 1992)

REC

# WANG XIAOBO

王小波 <sup>(1952–1997)</sup>

The perennial dark horse of modern Chinese literature, Wang Xiaobo is still a favorite with readers, but was never quite accepted by the official literary world. He thought of himself primarily as an author of fiction – most of which was published in his *Golden Age*, *Silver Age* and *Bronze Age* collections – but it was his essays on society, culture and art that first brought him prominence. The tone in which he wrote about Chinese society and culture seems light, and is often humorous, and his fiction often makes use of sexuality for subversive effect. This has given him a reputation for naughtiness, which has in part obscured the deep seriousness of his political commentary.

## Selected Works

NOVELS

*Geming Shiqi de Aiqing* 革命时期的爱情 (2008). Translated by Michæl Rodriguez and Wang Dun as *Love in an Age of Revolution* (MCLC Resource Center Publication, 2009)

*Huangjin Shidai* 黄金时代 (1999). Translated by Jason Sommer and Hongling Zhang as *Wang in Love and Bondage* (State University of

New York Press, 2007)

SHORT STORIES

*Jiujiu Qingren*舅舅情人 (In *Tangren Gushi* 唐人故事, 2006).
Translated by Eric Abrahamsen as 'Mister Lover' (Read Paper
Republic, 2015)

ESSAYS

*Chenmo de Daduoshu* 沉默的大多数 (in *Wode jingshen jiayuan* 我的
精神家园, 1997). Translated by Eric Abrahamsen as 'The Silent
Majority' (The Asia Literary Review, 2009)
A collection of Wang Xiaobo's essays in English is forthcoming from
Astra Books

REC

# WARRING YOUNG SEVEN
## 战七少

Warring Young Seven is the pen name of Zhang Yawei (张雅维). Born in Hebei Province, she now lives in Beijing. She began writing in 2015, and is best known for her online novels *The Anarchic Consort* (2015) and *National School Prince Is a Girl* (2017). Her novels contain strong elements of e-sports, yet their overriding theme is still romance. Zhang Yawei has said she wants to convey a sense of self-fulfillment, emphasizing that 'Self-esteem, self-love, and self-sufficiency are the guardian angels of young women.'

## Selected Works

NOVELS

*Guomin Xiaocao shi Nüsheng* 国民校草是女生 (2017). Translated by Hanyee Translations as *National School Prince Is a Girl* (webnovels.com)

*Shengshi Huangfei* 盛世凰妃 (2015). Translated by Nyoi-bo Studio, Misty Cloud Translations and Larber Studio as *The Anarchic Consort* (webnovels.com)

# WEI HUI

周卫慧 [(1973– )]

Zhou Weihui, more commonly known as Wei Hui, is a contemporary writer best known for her portrayal of China's post-70s generation, who grew up during the reform era that followed the death of Chairman Mao.

Born in Yuyao, Zhejiang Province, in 1973, Wei Hui grew up in a military family and studied Chinese literature at Shanghai's Fudan University. She made her literary debut in *Writer Magazine*, and in 1998 published her first collection of short stories, *Pistol of Desire*. However, it was the publication of *Shanghai Baby* that launched her into the public eye. The semi-autographical novel, which explicitly explores female sexuality, drug addiction, and mental illness, sold 11 million copies over a six-month period, before being banned by the Chinese government. Despite being labelled 'pornographic' and 'decadent' in China, *Shanghai Baby* quickly made waves in the West for its frank and revealing nature. First published in translation in 2000, the book is currently available in thirty-four languages.

In 2005, Wei Hui published *Marrying Buddha* (我的禪),

which was banned in China but subsequently translated for an international audience. In 2007, she published *Dog Dad* (狗爸爸). The same year, she suffered a serious spinal injury and has since taken an indefinite break from writing.

Wei Hui has been categorised as a 'glamorous writer' (*meinü zuojia* 美女作家), a disparaging label that has since been applied to many female writers as a way of devaluing their work. But her unflinching honesty in examining both her own life and her society has offered international readers a glimpse into how globalisation liberated and problematised women's lives.

## Selected Works

**NOVELS**

*Shanghai Baobei* 上海宝贝 (1999). Translated by Bruce Humes as *Shanghai Baby* (Simon & Schuster, 2001)

*Wo de Chan* 我的禪 (2005). Translated by Larissa Heinrich as *Marrying Buddha* (Little, Brown and Company, 2005)

ML

# WONG BIK WAN
黃碧雲 <sup>(1961  )</sup>

A graduate in journalism, criminology, and law, Wong Bik Wan worked as a reporter and scriptwriter before her career as an author picked up. Informed by her intimate knowledge of Hong Kong, her works often feature young women as principal characters and give voice to marginalised members of society. For instance, her early short story 'I'm a Woman, She's a Woman' (她是女子，我也是女子) explores desire, love, and loss in a relationship between two women. Many of Wong Bik Wan's stories also capture the darker and more violent aspects of human life, depicting brutality and abuse.

She has received many awards, notably for her short story collection *Tenderness and Violence* (溫柔與暴烈, not translated); for the novel *Portraits of Virtuous Women* (烈女圖, not translated), a bleak history of modern Hong Kong narrated through the lives of three generations of women; and for the novella *Memoirs of A Virtuous Man* (烈佬傳, not translated). In the latter, she blends Cantonese dialect with standard literary Chinese to recount a reformed gangster's experiences in the Wan Chai district underworld.

Her most recent work is the creative non-fiction *The Death of Lo Kei* (盧麒之死, 2018, untranslated), which investigates the mysterious death of a teenage leader during the 1966 peaceful demonstration that spiralled into violent clashes; his death was officially pronounced a suicide. Written a few years after Hong Kong's 2014 'Umbrella Revolution' protests and the subsequent 2016 Mong Kok Civil Unrest, the book reflects on individual sacrifice and collective guilt in social movements in Hong Kong.

Born in Hong Kong, Wong Bik Wan publishes in Hong Kong and Taiwan. She has chosen not to publish in mainland China, nor in simplified Chinese.

## Selected Works

**NOVELS**

*Doomsday Hotel* 末日酒店 (bilingual edition). (Cosmos天地圖書有限公司, 2011)

# XI XI
西西 <sup>(1938–)</sup>

Xi Xi is the pseudonym of author and poet Zhang Yan, one of Hong Kong's most popular and celebrated authors. She chose her pen name, she told *Literary Hub*, because it resembles the legs of a girl playing hopscotch. Xi Xi was born in Shanghai in 1938 but has lived in Hong Kong since 1950, and is the author of more than two dozen volumes of fiction, poetry and belles lettres.

Her 1979 work *My City* (我城), originally serialized in a local newspaper with Xi Xi's own illustrations, depicts a tapestry of Hong Kong life and is seen as a key work in the city's literary canon. Her subsequent novel, *Flying Carpet* (飞毯), also depicts Hong Kong's history and development over several generations. Other works are more personal, notably the stories collected in *A Girl Like Me* (像我这样的一个女子), and her 1992 novel *Mourning a Breast* (哀悼乳房), based on her own experience of breast cancer.

Xi Xi has also worked as a teacher, and served as editor of *Chinese Students Weekly*, *Thumb Weekly* and *Plain Leaf Literature*. Her essay, 'Shops' (店铺), an overview of life in a bustling corner of Hong Kong, is used as curriculum material by the Hong Kong Certificate of Education Examination. She was awarded the Newman Prize for Chinese Literature in 2019 and the Swedish Cikada Prize in 2020.

## Selected Works

**NOVELS**

*Feitan* 飞毯 (1996). Translated by Diana Yue as *Flying Carpet: A Tale of Fertillia* (Hong Kong University Press, 2000)
*Wocheng* 我城 (1979). Translated by Eva Hung as *My City: A Hong Kong Story* (Renditions Paperbacks, 1993)

**SHORT STORIES**

*Pingguo* 苹果. Translated by Jennifer Feeley as 'Apple' (*Words Without Borders*, 2018)
*Chen Dawen Banjia* 陈大文搬家 (2000). Translated by Steve Bradbury as 'Davin Chan Moves Out' (*Words Without Borders*, 2011)

**SHORT STORY COLLECTIONS**

*Fucheng Zhiguai* 浮城志异 (in *Fucheng 1.2.3——Xi Xi xiaoshuo xinxi* 浮城1.2.3.——西西小說新析, 2008) Translated by Eva Hung, John Dent-Young and Esther Dent-Young as *Marvels of a Floating City and Other Stories: An Authorized Collection* (Renditions Paperbacks, 1997)
*Xiang Wo Zheyang Yige Nüzi* 像我这样的一个女子. Translated by multiple translators as *A Girl Like Me and Other Stories* (Chinese University Press, 1988)

A NOVEL BY XI XI

Flying
Carpet
A Tale of Fertillia

*English Translation by Diana Yue*

# XIA JIA
## 夏笳 (1984– )

Ken Liu writes: "Xia Jia published her first short story, 'The Demon-Enslaving Flask,' in 2004 (English translation by Linda Rui Feng in the November 2012 issue of *Renditions*), when she was still a college student. The story, a sci-fi history in which 'Maxwell's demon' was a literal demon instead of a thought experiment, catapulted its author into the limelight by winning her a Galaxy Award for Best New Writer. At the same time, the story, which was published in the 'Twilight Zone' section of *Science Fiction World*, China's biggest science fiction magazine, 'spawned a series of heated debates about how (and whether) we should blur (or further defend) the boundary between science fiction and other genres,' according to Xia Jia.

Exploring the twilight frontier between worlds would become a constant theme in Xia Jia's career. Trained to be a physicist as an undergraduate, she switched to film studies and comparative literature for graduate school, where her PhD dissertation was titled 'Fear and Hope in the Age of Globalization: Contemporary Chinese Science Fiction and Its Cultural Politics (1991–2012)'. Her works are imbued with the tension between shifting tradition and revolutionary modernity, core and periphery, the written word and the moving image, rational analysis and intuitive recognition.

A multiple winner of the Galaxy and Nebula Awards for Chinese science fiction, Xia Jia is beloved by many fans and praised by fellow writers, but as a woman writer in a male-dominated field whose work defies easy categorization her stories have also continued to generate controversy." (An excerpt from Ken Liu's interview with Xia Jia in Clarkesworld issue 100, January 2015, reproduced by kind permission of the author. First published in *Clarkesworld*, http://clarkesworldmagazine.com/xia_interview/)

## Selected Works

SHORT STORY COLLECTIONS
*Spring Festival*, translated by Ken Liu (*Future Fiction*, 2015)
*A Summer Beyond Your Reach*, translated by Ken Liu, Carmen Yiling Yan, Emily Jin & Rebecca Kuang (Wyrm Publishing, 2021)

# XU XIAOBIN
徐小斌 [(1953– )]

Xu Xiaobin was born in Beijing and is one of China's leading twentieth-century female authors. Xu began publishing her fiction in the early 1980s, after spending time working in the countryside and at a factory in Heilongjiang during the Cultural Revolution. Her work focuses almost exclusively on women, depicting women's experiences and hardships in modern China. Alongside her career as an author, she is also a successful artist, and currently works as a screenplay writer.

Xu Xiaobin's most noted works are her three novels *Crystal Wedding* (水晶婚), *Feathered Serpent* (羽蛇), and *Dunhuang Dream* (敦煌遗梦), all of which have been translated into English. *Crystal Wedding* tells the story of a woman named Yang Tian, her unhappy marriage, and her fateful meeting with her first love in Tiananmen Square during the 1989 protests. *Feathered Serpent* tells the story of a woman trying to find love amidst China's political upheavals between 1950 and 1989. *Dunhuang Dream* tells the story of three women who visit Dunhuang in north-west China, and the unforeseen consequences of their trip to the

Mogao caves. A number of Xu's short stories have also been published by Balestier Press, including *Queen Bee and Other Stories* (2019) and *A Classical Tragedy* (2020).

Xu has received multiple prizes for her work, including the Lu Xun Prize, which she won in 1998. In 2015, the English translation of her novel *Crystal Wedding*, by Nicky Harman, won an English Pen Translates Award, and in 2016, it was longlisted for the Financial Times / Oppenheimer Emerging Voices Awards.

## Selected Works

### NOVELS

*Shuijing Hun* 水晶婚 (2016). Translated by Nicky Harman as *Crystal Wedding* (Balestier, 2016)

*Dunhuang Yimeng* 敦煌遗梦 (2007). Translated by John Balcom as *Dunhuang Dream* (Atria International, 2011)

*Yushe* 羽蛇 (2000). Translated by John Howard-Gibbon and Joanne Wang as *Feathered Serpent* (Simon and Schuster, 2009)

### SHORT STORY COLLECTIONS

*A Classical Tragedy: Short Stories* by Xu Xiaobin. Translated by Natascha Bruce and Nicky Harman (Balestier, 2020)

*Feng Hou* 蜂后 (1999). Translated by John Howard-Gibbon, Natascha Bruce, Nicky Harman and Alvin Leung as *Queen Bee and Other Stories* (Balestier, 2019)

### SHORT STORY

*Xue* 雪. Translated by Natascha Bruce and Nicky Harman as 'Snow' (Read Paper Republic, 2016)

AC

Crystal Wedding

A NOVEL

XU XIAOBIN

Translated by Nicky Harman

WINNER
ENGLISH PEN
AWARD

# XU XU
徐訏 <sup>(1908–1980)</sup>

Xu Xu was the pen name of Xu Boxu (徐伯訏), an important figure in modern Chinese literature. Born in Cixi in the coastal province of Zhejiang, south of Shanghai, he attended Peking University, where he studied Philosophy between 1927 and 1932. He then moved to Shanghai where he associated with the author Lin Yutang (1895–1976).

In 1936 Xu Xu went to Paris to further his studies. He returned to China during the second Sino-Japanese War, but in 1950 he left the newly founded People's Republic of China for Hong Kong, where he continued his writing and published dozens of short stories and novellas. He spent the rest of his life in Hong Kong, and taught in Chu Hai College, the Chinese University of Hong Kong and Baptist University; he also taught at Nanyang University in Singapore. As a writer, editor, and educator, Xu Xu has had a formative impact on the generation of post-war writers emerging in Hong Kong and Taiwan. His major works include the short story 'Ghost Love' and the novel *Whistling Wind* (1946).

# Selected Works

SHORT STORY COLLECTIONS

*Bird Talk and Other Stories by Xu Xu: Modern Tales of a Chinese Romantic.*
Translated by Frederik Green (Berkeley: Stone Bridge Press, 2020)

BBS

# XU ZECHEN
徐则臣 (1978– )

A native of Jiangsu Province, Xu Zechen obtained a Master's degree in Chinese Literature at Peking University and is now an editor at *People's Literature* magazine. Despite this pedigree, Xu's fiction is focused primarily on China's less-fortunate social classes, such as migrant workers or peddlers of pirated DVDs – and his spare, realist style lends some wry humor to their struggles.

Xu Zechen has published several novels such as *Running Through Beijing* and *Jerusalem.* He has won a number of prizes within China for new and promising writers and is generally considered one of the burgeoning new stars of China's literary scene. His latest novel, *Northwards* (*Bei Shang* 北上), was awarded the prestigious Mao Dun Literature Prize in 2019.

## Selected Works

NOVELS
*Yelusaleng* 耶路撒冷 (2014). Translated by David Haysom as *Jerusalem* (as yet unpublished)

*Paobu Chuanguo Zhongguancun* 跑步穿过中关村 (2008).
Translated by Eric Abrahamsen as *Running Through Beijing*
(Two Lines Press, 2014)

NOVELLAS

*Cang Sheng* 苍声 (2015). Translated by Charles Laughlin as
'Voice Change' in *By the River: Seven Contemporary Chinese Novellas*
(University of Oklahoma Press, 2016)

SHORT STORIES

*Shijian Jianshi* 时间简史 (2012). Translated by Eric Abrahamsen as 'A
Brief History of Time' (*n+1* magazine online, 2012)

*Benma* 奔马 (2012). Translated by Helen Wang as 'Galloping Horses'
(*The Guardian* online, China Stories, 2012)

*Qiying* 弃婴 (2005). Translated by Nicky Harman as 'Throwing Out
the Baby' (*Words without Borders*, 2012)

*Lunzi shi Yuande* 轮子是圆的. Translated by Eric Abrahamsen as
'Wheels Are Round' in *Shi Cheng: Stories from Urban China* (Comma
Press, 2012)

MG

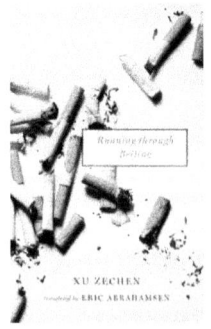

# XUE YIWEI
## 薛忆沩 <sup>(1964−)</sup>

Xue Yiwei was born in Chenzhou in Hunan Province and grew up in the city of Changsha. He currently lives in Montréal, Canada, where he has written more than twenty short stories and novels set in China. Shenzheners is a collection of short stories inspired by James Joyce's *Dubliners*, set in the modern city of Shenzhen in Guangdong Province, a stone's throw from Hong Kong. His latest novel, *King Lear and Nineteen Seventy-Nine* (李尔王与1979, untranslated) is about the Cultural Revolution.

As a writer, Xue Yiwei is interested in Chinese culture, especially the role of the individual in history. Before moving to Canada, he taught Chinese Literature at Shenzhen University. Xue has a BSc in Computer Science from Beijing University of Aeronautics and Astronautics, an MA in English Literature from Université de Montréal, and a PhD in Linguistics from Guangdong University of Foreign Studies.

## Selected Works

NOVELS

*Baiqiu'en de Haizimen* 白求恩的孩子们 (2011). Translated by Darryl Sterk as *Dr. Bethune's Children* (Linda Leith Publishing, 2017)

SHORT STORY COLLECTIONS

*Chuzuche Siji*出租车司机 (2016). Translated by Darryl Sterk as *Shenzheners* (Linda Leith Publishing, 2016)

*Chinese Literature and Culture Volume 5: Xue Yiwei and His War Stories* (2015). Translated by Chu Dongmei, Alison Sen Li, Liu Xiao, Fraser Sutherland, Craig Hulst, Caroline A. Brown, Stephen Nashef (CreateSpace Independent Publishing Platform, 2015)

# YAN GE
颜歌 (1984– )

Yan Ge was born in Sichuan Province. Her first short story collection was published in China when she was seventeen. Yan Ge's early works focused on the wonders, gods and ghosts of Chinese myth and made her especially popular with teenagers. The novel *May Queen* (五月女王, not translated) saw her break through as a critically acclaimed author, writing realist, Sichuan-based fiction, by turns sharp, funny and touching. Her Chinese writing employs colourful Sichuan dialect as well as standard Chinese.

Yan Ge is the author of thirteen books, including five novels. She has received numerous awards and was named by *People's Literature* magazine as one of twenty Future Literature Masters in China. Her work has been translated into eleven languages, including English, French and German. The English translation of her novel *The Chilli Bean Paste Clan* (我们家) was published in 2018, and her *Strange Beasts of China* (异兽志) came out in English in 2020. Both won English PEN Translates Awards. Her novella *White Horse* (HopeRoad, 2019) was shortlisted for the Warwick Prize for Women in Translation 2020. She was on the judging panel of the International Dublin Literary Award 2019.

Yan writes in English as well as Chinese. Her English writing has appeared in the *New York Times*, the *Irish Times*, *TLS*, the *Stinging Fly* and elsewhere. She has an MFA in Creative Writing from the University of East Anglia where she was the recipient of the UEA International Award 2018/19. Her English language debut short story collection *Elsewhere* will be published by Faber in the UK and Scribner in the USA in spring 2023, followed by a novel, *Hotel Destination*. Yan lives in Norwich with her husband and son.

## Selected Works

**NOVELS**

*Yi Shou Zhi* 异兽志 (2008). Translated by Jeremy Tiang as *Strange Beasts of China* (Tilted Axis Press/Melville House, 2020)

*Women Jia* 我们家. Translated by Nicky Harman as *The Chilli Bean Paste Clan* (Balestier Press, 2018)

**NOVELLAS**

*Baima* 白马. Translated by Nicky Harman as *White Horse* (HopeRoad, 2019)

**SHORT STORIES**

*Ronghua Shou* 荣华兽. Translated by Jeremy Tiang as 'Flourishing Beasts' in *That We May Live: Speculative Chinese Fiction* (Two Lines Press, 2020)

*Sanyi Chahui* 三一茶会. Translated by Karmia Olutade as 'We Meet at Twilight' in *Pathlight 14* (2016)

*Zhong Nige* 钟腻哥. Translated by Nicky Harman as 'Sissy Zhong' in *Paper Republic* (2015)

*Pingle Shi* 平乐事. Translated by Poppy Toland as 'The Spices of Life', in *Los Angeles Review of Books (LARB) China Channel* (2018)

FB

# YAN GELING
嚴歌苓 (1958–)

Born in Shanghai, Yan Geling is one of the most acclaimed contemporary novelists and screenwriters writing in the Chinese language today, as well as a well-established writer in English. She is the author of numerous novels, short stories, essays and screenplays. Many of her works have been adapted for film and television.

Yan began performing as a dancer at the age of twelve. She served in a performance troupe in the People's Liberation Army (PLA) in the Chengdu Military District during the Cultural Revolution and frequently toured Tibet. She later served as a journalist near the front of the Sino-Vietnamese Border War. She was subsequently assigned to a writers' unit under the PLA Railway Engineering Corps and achieved a rank equivalent to lieutenant colonel.

Yan Geling's first novel was published in 1985. She has written in both Chinese and English: *The Banquet Bug* (published as *The Uninvited* in the United Kingdom, 2006) was written in English, while *Fusang* (扶桑), as well as a collection of stories entitled *White Snake and Other Stories*

(白蛇), and many subsequent novels were written in Chinese and translated (see below).

Yan Geling is notable among Chinese authors for having close links with the film industry. She is a member of the Academy of Motion Pictures Arts and Sciences and of the Writers' Guild of America, west, the Hollywood screenwriters' union. Many of her works have been adapted for film and television, often with Yan writing the screenplays herself. These include *Xiu Xiu: The Sent-Down Girl*, directed by Joan Chen, and *Youth* 芳华, directed by Feng Xiaogang. Zhang Yimou adapted her novel *13 Flowers of Nanjing* (金陵十三钗) to the screen as *The Flowers of War*, while his movies *Coming Home* and *One Second* are based on Yan's novel *The Criminal Lu Yanshi*.

### Selected Works

NOVELS

*Miyuzhe* 密语者. Translated by Jeremy Tiang as *The Secret Talker* (HarperVia, 2021)

*Xiaoyi Duohe* 小姨多鹤 (2008). Translated by Esther Tyldesley as *Little Aunt Crane* (Harvill Secker, 2015)

*Jinling Shisan Chai* 金陵十三钗 (2011). Translated by Nicky Harman as *The Flowers of War* (Vintage, 2012)

*The Banquet Bug: A Novel* (Hyperion, 2006). Written in English. Published as *The Uninvited* in UK (Faber and Faber, 2006).

*Fusang* 扶桑. Translated by Cathy Silber as *The Lost Daughter of Happiness* (Hachette Books, 2001)

SHORT STORIES

*Nü Fangdong* 女房东. Translated by Lawrence A. Walker as 'The

Landlady' in *Granta* (2015)

*Mage Shi Zuo Cheng: Peiqian Huo* 妈阁是座城: 赔钱货 (2014).
Excerpt translated by David Haysom as 'Disappointing Returns' in
*Read Paper Republic* (2015)

*Mai Hong Pingguo de Mang Nüzi* 卖红苹果的盲女子. Translated
by Herbert Batt as 'The Blind Woman Selling Red Apples' in *Tales
of Tibet: Sky Burials, Prayer Wheels, and Wind Horses.* (Rowman and
Littlefield, 2001)

NOVELLA AND SHORT STORY COLLECTIONS
*Bai She* 白蛇 . Translated by Lawrence A. Walker as *White Snake and
Other Stories* (Aunt Lute Books, 1999)

ESSAYS
*Man Man Man* 瞒瞒瞒. Translated by Nicky Harman as 'Hide! Hide!
Hide!' (Read Paper Republic, 2020)

BOOKS TO FILMS
Film name: *One Second* (2020) Director: Zhang Yimou. Adapted from
*The Criminal Lu Yanshi* 陆犯焉识 (2011).
Film name: *A City Called Macau* (2018) Director: Li Shaohong.
Adapted from *A City Called Macau* 妈阁是座城 (2014).
Film name: *Youth* (2017) Director: Feng Xiaogang. Adapted from
*Fanghua* 芳华 (2017).
Film name: *Coming Home* (2014). Director: Zhang Yimou. Adapted
from *The Criminal Lu Yanshi* 陆犯焉识 (2011).
Film name: *Xiu Xiu: The Sent-down Girl* (1998). Director: Joan Chen.
Adapted from *Celestial Bath* 天浴 (1996).
Film name: *Siao Yu* (1995). Director: Sylvia Chang. Script by Sylvia
Chang and Ang Lee and co-produced by Ang Lee. Adapted from
*Xiaoyu* 少女小渔 (1992).
Yan Geling's filmography can also be found by searching on IMDb.
com (International Movie Database)

# YAN LIANKE
阎连科 (1958- )

Renowned Chinese novelist Yan Lianke was born in impoverished Song County, Henan Province. His parents were illiterate farmers who lacked the means to send him to university. Instead, they encouraged him to enlist in the army, where he rose through the ranks and eventually became a propaganda writer. Upon returning to civilian life, Yan embarked on a career as a novelist. His writing career started in 1978 and in the decades since, he has produced an extensive body of work that ranges from novels, novellas and short fiction to essays and criticism.

His work is highly satirical, which has resulted in some of his most renowned works being banned. His most acclaimed works include: *Dream of Ding Village* (丁庄梦), a tale of the blood trade and subsequent AIDS epidemic in a rural Henan village; *Lenin's Kisses* (受活), a sweeping tale of the lives of disabled rural villagers, from the Chinese Communist revolution through the years of reform and opening up; and *Serve the People* (为人民服务), which was banned in China and later translated into English, French, and Japanese.

Among many accolades, he has been awarded the Franz Kafka Prize, and received two of China's most prestigious literary honours, the Lu Xun Prize and the Lao She Award. In 2020, he was announced as the winner of the Newman Prize for Chinese Literature, 2021.

## Selected Works

NOVELS

*Si Shu* 四书 (2011). Translated by Carlos Rojas as *The Four Books* (shortlisted for the 2016 Man Booker International Prize, Grove Atlantic, 2015)

*Shouhuo* 受活 (2004). Translated by Carlos Rojas as *Lenin's Kisses* (Grove Atlantic, 2012)

*Dingzhuang Meng* 丁庄梦 (2006). Translated by Cindy M. Carter as *Dream of Ding Village* (Grove Atlantic, 2011)

*Wei Renmin Fuwu* 为人民服务 (2005). Translated by Julia Lovell as *Serve the People!* (Grove Atlantic, 2008)

NOVELLAS

*Balou Tian Ge* 耙耧天歌 (2014). Translated by Carlos Rojas as *Marrow* (Penguin China, 2015)

NOVELLA COLLECTIONS

*The Years, Months Days*. Translated by Carlos Rojas (Grove Press, 2017)

MG

# YANG LIAN
杨炼 (1955–)


Born in Bern, Switzerland in 1955 to diplomat parents, and raised in Beijing, Yang Lian is one of the most prolific contemporary Chinese poets, well-represented in translation. He started writing poetry while he was labouring in the countryside during the Cultural Revolution. Later, he became a founding member of the group of 'Misty Poets', along with Bei Dao, Gu Cheng, Mang Ke, Duo Duo, Shu Ting and others, publishing his works in *Jintian* (Today) magazine in the late 1970s. An outspoken advocate of political and artistic freedom, Yang was living in New Zealand as a visiting scholar at the time of the Tiananmen protests in 1989, and was subsequently exiled from China after organizing protests against the Chinese government in Auckland.

Yang Lian now has both New Zealand and British citizenship, and has held various international fellowships and guest professorships in the United States, Germany, Italy, Taiwan, and Australia. He was instrumental in establishing the Independent Chinese PEN Center in 2001. He has won many Chinese and international prizes including the English PEN Award, the International Nonino Prize in Italy, and the Shanghai Literature Magazine Prize for Poetry. In 2021 he and translator Brian Holton won the inaugural Sarah Maguire Prize for Poetry.

Yang Lian's works are strongly influenced by classical Chinese poetry, alongside many creative and inventive elements of his own. His best-known works include: *Dead in Exile* (流亡的死者, 1990), *Where the Sea Stands Still* (大海停止之处, 1999), *Concentric Circles* (同心圆, 2005), *Anniversary Snow* (周年之雪, 2019), winner of the inaugural Sarah Maguire Prize for Poetry in Translation in 2021, and the autobiographical *Narrative Pœm* (叙事诗, 2017). Yang Lian's own Chinese translations of George Orwell's *1984* and *Animal Farm* were published in Taiwan in 2020. He currently lives in London and Berlin, and is married to writer and artist YoYo (Liu Youhong).

## Selected Works

POETRY COLLECTIONS

*Mianju Yu Eyu* 面具与鳄鱼. Translated by Mabel Lee as *Masks and Crocodile* (Wild Peony, 1990)

*Liumang de Sizhe* 流亡的死者. Translated by Mabel Lee as *The Dead in Exile* (Tiananmen Publications, 1990)

*Wu Ren Cheng* 无人称. Translated by Brian Holton as *Non-Person Singular* (Wellsweep Press, 1994)

*Dahai Tingzhi Zhi Chu* 大海停止之处. Translated by Brian Holton as *Where the Sea Stands Still* (Bloodaxe Books, 1999)

*Xingfu Guihun Shouji* 幸福鬼混手记. Translated by Brian Holton as *Notes of a Blissful Ghost* (Renditions Paperbacks, 2002)

*Tongxin Yuan* 同心圆. Translated by Brian Holton and Agnes Hung-

Chong Chan as *Concentric Circles* (Bloodaxe Books, 2005)

*Huanxiang Zhong de Chengshi* 幻象中的城市. Translated by Hilary Chung and Jacob Edmond as *Unreal City* (Auckland University Press, 2006)

*Qicheng Shuangyuzuo* 启程双鱼座. Translated by Brian Holton as *Riding Pisces* (Shearsman Books, 2008)

*Li Hegu de Shi* 李河谷的诗. Translated by Brian Holton and Agnes Hung-Chong Chan as *Lee Valley Pœms* (Bloodaxe Books, 2009)

*Dahai de Di San An* 大海的第三岸. Translated by W.N. Herbert as *The Third Shore* (Shearsman Books, 2013)

*Pangda de Danshu* 庞大的单数. Translated by Brian Holton as *A Massively Single Number* (Shearsman Books, 2015)

*Xushi Shi* 叙事诗. Translated by Brian Holton as *Narrative Pœm* (Bloodaxe Books, 2017)

*Zhounian Zhi Xue* 周年之雪. Translated by Brian Holton, W.N. Herbert, L. Leigh, Liang Lizhen, Pascale Petit, Fiona Sampson, George Szirzes, and Joshua Weiner as *Anniversary Snow* (Shearsman Books, 2019)

SHORT STORIES

*Gui Hua* 鬼话. Translated by Charles Laughlin as 'Ghost Talk' (Running Wild, 1994)

AG

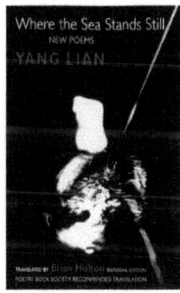

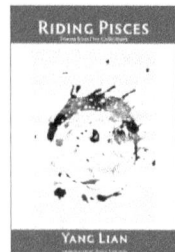

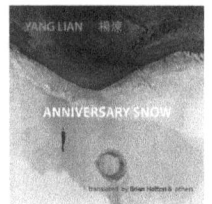

# YIN LICHUAN
尹丽川 (1973– )

Born in Chongqing, Yin Lichuan is an independent filmmaker, author, and poet. She studied French at Peking University, before pursuing a graduate degree in filmmaking at the École Supérieure Libre d'Etudes Cinématographiques (ESEC) in Paris. She is a founder of the 'Lower Body' (下半身) poetry movement, established in Beijing in the early 2000s.

In 2001, Yin published the poetry collection *A Little More Comfortable* (再舒服一些, not yet translated); and her novel *Bitch* (贱人, not yet translated) appeared the following year. Her poetry collection *Karma* (因果, translated by Fiona Sze-Lorrain) was published in English in 2020.

In 2006, Yin turned to filmmaking and wrote and directed her first film, *Chinese Father* (公园, also known as *The Park*) to great international acclaim. In 2008, her second film, *Knitting* (牛郎织女), was selected for the Director's Fortnight at the Cannes International Film Festival. In 2020, she co-wrote and co-directed the film *Hear Her Speak* (听见她说).

## Selected Works

PŒTRY

*Yin Guo* 因果. Translated by Fiona Sze-Lorrain as *Karma: Pœms* (Tolsun Books, 2020)

*Pœms by Yin Lichuan*. Translated by Steve Bradbury (Jacket2, 2011)

*Selected Pœms*. Translated by Xiao Cheng (Wasafiri, 2008)

AG

# YU HUA
余华 (1960– )

Now one of China's best-known novelists, Yu Hua was initially assigned to a job as a dentist and began writing in 1980 to escape the monotony of his work. In the early stages of his career, he was seen as one of China's leading 'avant-garde' writers (alongside authors such as Mo Yan, Can Xue, Su Tong and Ge Fei). His experimental works were filled with absurd and satirical descriptions, sometimes violent and bloody.

In the 1990s, Yu Hua´s writing style changed, as he switched to a more realistic approach and employed simpler language and techniques. These stories were usually about ordinary people and set in the countryside. In 1993, his breakthrough novel *To Live* (活着), depicting the traumatic experiences of a married couple from the 1940s to the Cultural Revolution, hit the bookshelves; its success was consolidated by the release the following year of Zhang Yimou's movie adaptation, starring Gong Li and Ge You. *To Live* was followed two years later by *Chronicles of a Blood Merchant* (许三观卖血记).

Yu Hua's more recent novels represent another new departure: *Brothers* (兄弟, 2005) is an ambitious epic about two step-brothers that blends the absurd and the tragic, while *The Seventh Day* (第七天,2015) is a dark look at the plight of China's underclasses. His 2010 essay collection, *China In Ten Words* (十个词汇里的中国), meanwhile, combines memoirs of his childhood amidst the violence and tumult of the Cultural Revolution, with acerbic social and political commentary on contemporary China. Banned in mainland China, it was well received in Taiwan and internationally.

Yu Hua is the recipient of numerous international awards and honours, including the James Joyce Award, Italy's Premio Grinzane Cavour and Giuseppe Acerbi prizes, and the French Prix Courrier International. In 2004 he was made a Chevalier de l'Ordre des Arts et des Lettres by the French government. In 2008, *Brothers* was shortlisted for the Man Asian Literary Prize.

## Selected Works

**NOVELS**

*Diqi Tian* 第七天 (2013). Translated by Allan Barr as *The Seventh Day* (Anchor, 2015)

*Xiongdi* 兄弟 (2005). Translated by Eileen Cheng-yin Chow and Carlos Rojas as *Brothers* (Picador, 2009)

*Xu Sanguan Maixie Ji* 许三观卖血记 (1995). Translated by Andrew Jones as *Chronicle of a Blood Merchant* (Anchor, 2004)

*Huozhe* 活着 (1993). Translated by Michæl Berry as *To Live* (Anchor, 2003)

SHORT STORY COLLECTIONS

*The April 3rd Incident*, by Allan Barr (Pantheon, 2018)

*Boy in the Twilight: Stories of the Hidden China.* Translated by Allan Barr (Anchor, 2014)

*The Past and the Punishments.* Translated by Andrew Jones (UH Press, 1996)

ESSAY COLLECTION

*Shige Cihui li de Zhongguo* 十个词汇里的中国 (2010) Translated by Allan Barr as *China in Ten Words* (Pantheon, 2011)

MG

# YU XIUHUA
余秀华 [(1976– )]

Yu Xiuhua is a Chinese poet who became famous after sharing her poetry on the Internet. She grew up in a small village and her childhood was not easy: Yu suffers from congenital cerebral palsy, which makes it difficult for her to speak and move around. Because of this, she could not help her parents with farm work, nor finish her high school studies. Poetry became her main focus and in 1998, when she was twelve, she wrote her first poem, 'Imprinting' (印痕, not yet translated).

At the age of nineteen, her parents arranged for her to marry a man twelve years older than her. However, the marriage was an unhappy one and, as soon as she could and in the teeth of considerable opposition from her family and the community, she filed for divorce. (Chinese women of course have a legal right to divorce, but this is still frowned upon in conservative rural areas.)

The poem that made her famous, 'Crossing Half of China to Sleep with You' (穿过大半个中国去睡你, 2018), first appeared on the author´s personal blog in 2014. The poem talks openly about sex, love, and desire and was an overnight sensation on the Chinese social media platform, Wechat.

In 2015, Yu had two best-selling poetry collections published: *The Moonlight Falls On My Left Hand* (月光落在左手上), and *Still Tomorrow* (摇摇晃晃的人间, not yet translated). Her third collection, *We Loved and Then Forgot* (我们爱过又忘记, not translated) came out in 2016. In the same year, Yu won the national prize for rural writers, 'Peasant Literature Award' (农民文学奖).

The major themes of her poems include love (or lack thereof), desire, the hardships of village life and her life with disabilities. In 2016, the Chinese movie director Fan Jian produced a documentary about Yu's life and career, *Still Tomorrow* (摇摇晃晃的人间).

## Selected Works

POEMS AND ESSAYS

*Moonlight Rests on My Left Palm*, translated by Fiona Sze-Lorrain (Astra House, 2021)

POEMS

*Chuanguo Dabange Zhongguo Qu Shui Ni* 穿过大半个中国去睡你 (2018). Translated by Ming Di as 'Crossing Half of China to Sleep with You' (*World Literature Today online*, 2018)
*Zai Daguchang Shang Gan Ji* 在打谷场上赶鸡 (2018). Translated by Ming Di as 'On the Threshing Floor, I Chase Chickens Away' (*World Literature Today online*, 2018)

TH

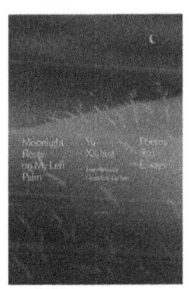

# ZHAI YONGMING

翟永明 (1955– )

Zhai Yongming was born in Chengdu, Sichuan province, and is a graduate of its University of Electronic Science and Technology. Chengdu is still her home and, in 1998, she opened the book and wine bar, White Nights (白夜酒吧), in the Nanfangcao district of the city. The bar, which she still runs, has become a noted venue for literary and artistic events.

Zhai Yongming is one of China's preeminent contemporary poets, consistently outspoken on the position of women in the Chinese literary world. Her first poetry collection, *Women* (*Nüren* 女人), was published in 1986. She has since published seven more collections of her poetry, and six volumes of essays and articles. Her work has been translated into English, French, Dutch, Italian, and German: translated volumes include *Changing Rooms* (2012), *Das Kaffeehauslied* (German), and *La Conscience de la Mort* (French). She was one of the participants in Interviews with Chinese Women Writers, published in October 2020 in Paper-Republic.org.

## Selected Works

POETRY COLLECTIONS

*The Changing Room: Selected Poetry of Zhai Yongming*, translated by Andrea Lingenfelter (Zephyr Press, 2012)

# ZHANG AILING (a.k.a. Eileen Chang)
张爱玲 <sup>(1920–1995)</sup>

Zhang Ailing is one of the best-known Chinese novelists, beloved by fans in mainland China, Taiwan and Hong Kong, and, in the years since her death in 1995, increasingly well known internationally. Several of her works have been adapted for the big screen, with *Lust, Caution* (色，戒), directed by Ang Lee, winning widespread critical acclaim internationally following its release in 2007.

Born in Shanghai into a wealthy family (she was a great-granddaughter of the late Qing Dynasty statesman Li Hongzhang), Zhang attended the English language girls' school St. Mary's Hall. Her childhood was not an easy one, however, with conflict between her parents, who eventually divorced. As a teenager, Zhang later clashed with her stepmother and opium addict father, who at one point beat her and locked her in her room for several months, before she fled to stay with her mother and aunt. In 1939, she embarked on a degree in English Literature at Hong Kong University (having been unable to take up a scholarship at the University of London due to the war in Europe.) She was in Hong Kong when the city fell to the Japanese military in December 1941. She later returned to Shanghai, then also under Japanese occupation, and quickly found success as a writer, with the publication of a number of essays, short stories and novels, notably *Love in a Fallen City* (傾城之戀, 1943), set in Hong Kong after the Japanese takeover, and the family saga *Golden Cangue* (金鎖記, 1943). Zhang herself wrote the screenplay for a 1950 movie adaptation of the latter, and also wrote a number of original screenplays while in Shanghai, including *Long Live the Missus* (*Taitai Wan Sui* 太太萬歲, 1947), a well-known satirical comedy about relationships between men and women.

Zhang was praised for the maturity and frankness of her writing about family and romantic relationships, and seen as a symbol of the modern, independent Shanghai woman. But after the Communist takeover in 1949, and having endured the collapse of her first marriage to the politician Hu Lancheng (denounced as a traitor for serving in the pro-Japanese puppet government), she left China in 1952. She went first to Hong Kong and then, in 1955, to the USA, where she settled, marrying American writer Ferdinand Reyher in 1956 and obtaining American citizenship in 1960.

Zhang continued to write during the 1950s, producing some of her best-known works, including *The Rice Sprout Song* (秧歌), which was originally written in English, and *Naked Earth* (赤地之恋). In the US, she later worked on several autobiographical novels, including the *Fall of the Pagoda*, originally written in English (1963). She also continued to write film scripts for the Hong Kong movie industry (including several comedies) until the mid-1960s.

In later years she taught and researched in a number of US universities, and also worked on an English translation of Han Bangqing's late Qing novel, *The Sing-song Girls of Shanghai* (海上花列傳, also known as *Flowers of Shanghai*). This was published after her death.

While Zhang Ailing did not achieve major commercial success in the west during her lifetime, her writing enjoyed a revival in popularity in Hong Kong and Taiwan in the 1960s and 70s, and from the 1980s in mainland China, as the nation re-opened to the outside world. Nevertheless, she never returned to China, and became increasingly reclusive in her later years, living alone following the death of her husband in 1967. She was found dead in her apartment in Los Angeles in 1995.

Zhang Ailing's continuing popularity lies in her vivid depiction of cosmopolitan life in Shanghai and Hong Kong, and her understanding of human relationships. Her writing has been described as 'cinematic and sensuous', with her works often focusing on love and betrayal, and the effects of war and turmoil on everyday life. A prolific writer, marked by the tragedies she witnessed and endured in her own life, Zhang has secured her place in the canon of Chinese literature.

## Selected Works

NOVELS

*Ban Sheng Yuan* 半生緣 , translated as *Half a Lifelong Romance* by Karen S. Kingsbury (Penguin Classics, 2014)

*Se, Jie* 色，戒 , translated by Julia Lovell as *Lust, Caution* (Penguin Classics, 2007)

SHORT STORIES

*Qing Cheng zhi Lian* 傾城之戀 , translated by Karen S. Kingsbury as *Love in a Fallen City* (Penguin Classics, 2007)

ESSAYS

*Liu Yan* 流言 , translated by Andrew F. Jones as *Written on Water* (New York Review of Book, 2021)

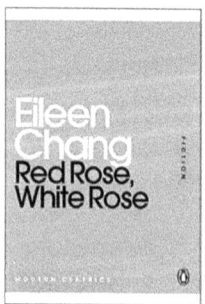

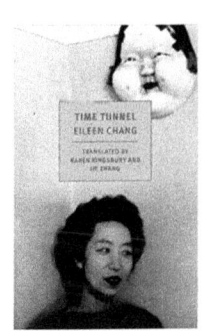

# ZHANG CHENGZHI

张承志 [(1948– )]

Zhang Chengzhi was born to Hui (Chinese Muslim) parents originally from Shandong province and is often named as the most influential Muslim writer in China. He began his writing career in 1978 and has been seen as a leading exponent of Chinese 'root-seeking literature' (寻根文学), even though he himself dismisses the concept. His work repeatedly touches on themes of martyrdom, enduring tradition, and resistance to materialism and urban life. Unlike many authors who lived through the Cultural Revolution and regret the chaos it created in their lives, Zhang's early works exhibit a noticeable idealism about his time as a Red Guard, and clearly demonstrate his desire to rebut the presumptions of 'scar literature' 伤痕文学 (the genre which emerged in the late 1970s and portrayed the sufferings of educated people during the Cultural Revolution).

The early 1980s have been described as Zhang's lyrical phase, and he became known as one of China's first practitioners of stream of consciousness fiction. In 1984, he quit his job at the China Writers' Association and moved to

China's Northwest, where he spent six years living among the Muslim community of Xihaigu in Ningxia. His time there resulted in his conversion to Islam and the completion of his most famous novel *History of the Soul* (心灵史). This work of narrative historical fiction explores personal and religious conflicts during more than a century and a half of development among the Jahriyya, a tariqah (or school of Sufism) in Northwestern China, and is interwoven with his own observations.

## Selected Works

**NOVELS**

*Xinling Shi* 心灵史 *History of the Soul* (not translated, 1991)

**NOVELLAS**

*Hei Junma* 黑骏马 (1981). Translated by Stephen Fleming as *The Black Steed: Three Novellas* (Panda, 1990)

**ESSAYS**

*Tiandao Liqiu* 天道立秋. Translated by Helen Wang as 'The Way of Heaven: Beginning of Autumn' in *Under-Sky Underground: Chinese Writing Today* (Wellsweeep, 1994)

MG

# ZHANG JIE
张洁 [(1937– )]

Zhang Jie was raised by her mother, a primary school teacher of Manchurian royal blood, in a village in Liaoning province. The invasion of the Japanese Imperial Army into Manchuria forced them to flee to Henan province. Thanks to her mother´s profession, Zhang learnt about classical Chinese literature; however, she also fell in love with Western literary masterpieces, especially the works of Dostoyevsky, Tolstoy and Twain.

At the age of 18, Zhang Jie entered Renmin University in Beijing, majoring in economics. During the years of the Cultural Revolution, she was criticized for being under the spell of 'poisonous' Western literature, and was sent to work on a prison farm in Jiangxi province, where she stayed for four years. When she later returned to Beijing after the death of Mao in 1976, she began her career as a writer.

Her first work was a collection of five short stories and two novellas set in China after the Cultural Revolution, *Love Must Not Be Forgotten* (爱，是不能忘记的). Published in 1979 and subsequently translated into many languages, this work challenged traditional Chinese views on marriage, and, as a result, was criticized for 'undermining socialist morality.' The collection takes its name from the eponymous novella, which tells the story of a daughter who discovers her mother's diary after the latter's death. In its pages, she learns about her mother´s love for an already married government official. Seeing that her mother's love was unfulfilled but also full of passion, the daughter decides to reject a proposal from a man she does not love, thus going against current social norms and expectations. Despite the criticism, the novel won a national book award, and served as the starting point for Zhang Jie´s change of career, from economist to a full-time writer.

In 1980, her novel *Leaden Wings* (沉重的翅膀) was published. The novel critiques the modernization of China´s economy, reflecting Zhang Jie's belief that China's rapid economic reforms should be balanced by social and political reforms. It was criticized for being anti-party and anti-socialist. However, in 1985, *Leaden Wings* received the prestigious Mao Dun Literature Prize.

In 1981, Zhang Jie´s novella, 'The Ark' (方舟, translated by Gladys Yang), was published. Considered at the time to be the first Chinese feminist novella, it tells the story of three career women – a writer, a translator and a film director – who refuse to be dependent on their husbands and leave their homes to live together. The story highlighted contemporary social problems in urban China, tackling themes such as divorce, sexual harassment in the workplace and inequality between men and women, as well as artistic freedom.

In 2005, Zhang Jie received the Mao Dun Literature Prize for a second time, for her trilogy *Wordless* (无字, not yet translated, 2002), which chronicles the story of several generations of women in one family and took her more than ten years to write.

## Selected Works

**NOVELS**
*Chenzhong De Chibang* 沉重的翅膀 (1987). Translated by Howard Goldblatt as *Heavy Wings* (Grove Weidenfeld, 1989) and by Gladys Yang as *Leaden Wing* (Virago Press, 1987)

**NOVELLAS**
*Fangzhou*方舟 (1981). Translated by Gladys Yang as 'The Ark' in *Love Must Not Be Forgotten* (China Books & Periodicals, 1986)

**SHORT STORY COLLECTIONS**
*Zhiyao Wu Shi Fasheng, Renhe Shi Dou Bu Hui Fasheng* 只要无事发生，任何事都不会发生 , (1988). Translated by Gladys Yang as *As Long as Nothing Happens Nothing Will* (Virago, 1988)
*Ai, Shi Buneng Wangji De* 爱，是不能忘记的 (1979). Translated by Gladys Yang as *Love Must Not Be Forgotten* (China Books & Periodicals, 1986)

TH

# ZHANG KANGKANG
张抗抗 <sup>(1950–)</sup>

Zhang Kangkang was born into a family of intellectuals in Hangzhou, and was strongly affected by events during the Cultural Revolution. As an educated urban youth, she was sent to a remote village in northeast China at the age of nineteen, to be 're-educated' by peasants and do manual labour. After Mao Zedong's death, Zhang was able to return to urban life and education. In 1977 she entered the Drama Department in Heilongjiang Art School. In 1979, she became a full-time writer with the Writers' Association of Heilongjiang.

Her first short story, *The Lamp* (灯, not yet translated), came out in 1972, and describes the lives of Chinese students sent to rural areas. Many of the youths who had been affected by the Cultural Revolution decided to write about their experiences. A new type of literature was born, known as 'scar' literature (*shanghen wenxue* 伤痕文学), with Zhang Kangkang as one of its leading figures.

In 1979, Zhang published her first novel, *The Right to Love* (爱的权力), a manifesto for the freedom of the individual. But it was *The Invisible Companion* (隐形伴侣, 1986), which brought her to wider public attention, with its focus on the state of mind and thought processes of the main characters. Using flashbacks and stream of consciousness, Zhang suggested that there was an invisible 'partner' within human beings, and pointed to the split personalities of 'educated youth' whose life had been shaped by propagandistic lies.

She won the Second Chinese Women´s Literature Award for her 2003 novel, *Uproarious Women* (作女, not yet translated), about strong creative women who are not afraid to live their lives in new ways. She used her own friends as prototypes for characters in the novel.

Zhang Kangkang has also published, novellas, short stories and memoirs, together with many essays. She is married to another Chinese writer, Jiang Rong (姜戎, 1946– ), author of *Wolf Totem* (狼图腾).

## Selected Works

NOVELS

*Yinxing Banlü* 隐形伴侣 (1986). Translated by Daniel Bryant as *The Invisible Companion* (New World Press, 1996)

*Ai De Quanli* 爱的权力 (1979). Translated by R.A. Roberts and Angela Knox as 'The Right to Love' in *One Half of the Sky: Selections from Contemporary Women Writers* (Heinemann, 1987)

NOVELLA

*Canren* 残忍 (2003). Translated by Richard King as 'Cruelty' in *Renditions* (The Chinese University of Hong Kong, 2003)

# ZHANG XIANLIANG

张贤亮 [(1936–2014)]

Zhang Xianliang was a writer of novels, poetry and essays, who was born into a middle-class family in Nanjing. After the Communist Party's victory in China's civil war in 1949, his father, a businessman and official of the defeated Kuomintang party, was accused of espionage and imprisoned. At around this time, when he was thirteen, Zhang Xianliang started to write poems.

During the Anti-Rightist Movement in 1957, Zhang's poems, especially the 'Song of the Great Wind' (大风歌, not translated), were criticized as being counter-revolutionary, rightist, and 'deviant'. He was sent to prison, and was later moved to a labour camp in Ningxia, northwest China, when he was twenty-one years old. When the Cultural Revolution began some nine years later, Zhang was viewed as a counter-revolutionary and 'revisionist'. He spent a total of twenty-two years either in prison or in labour camps.

After his release, Zhang became a major figure in the 'scar literature' movement, which depicted the experiences of young people who had been sent down to the countryside for 're-education', or had otherwise suffered, during the Cultural Revolution. His best-known work, the autobiographical novel *Half of Man is Woman* (男人的一半是女人, 1985) reflects his experiences in the Cultural Revolution and the impact these had on his life. Their effect on his sexual life is a central theme of the book – and the representation of the central character's sexual impotence in the novel is also a metaphor for the more profoundly troubling impotence of China's intellectuals, a theme that aroused controversy in China.

Zhang's experiences in labour camps are also depicted in the novel *My Bodhi Tree* (我的菩提树, 1997) which is based on a secret diary that he kept during his imprisonment. Apart from his life as a writer, Zhang also served as president of the Writers' Association of Ningxia, and was the founder of the West China Film Studios, where some of China's most famous movies were filmed.

## Selected Works

NOVELS:

*Wo De Puti Shu* 我的菩提树 (1997). Translated by Martha Avery as *My Bodhi Tree* (Minerva, 1997)

*Xiguan Siwang* 习惯死亡 (1991). Translated by Martha Avery as *Getting Used to Dying* (Harper Collins, 1991)

*Nanren De Yiban Shi Nüren* 男人的一半是女人 (1985). Translated by Martha Avery as *Half of Man is Woman* (W.W. Norton, 1988)

NONFICTION:

*Fannao Jiushi Zhihui* 烦恼就是智慧 (1995). Translated by Martha Avery as *Grass Soup* (Secker & Warburg, 1995)

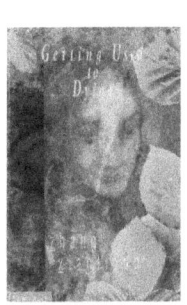

# ZHANG YUERAN
张悦然 (1982– )

Zhang Yueran is regarded as one of China's most influential young writers. She began writing at the age of fourteen, and won first prize in the nationwide New Concept Writing Competition while still a high school student. She later studied English and law at Shandong University, completed a graduate degree in computer science at National University of Singapore, and holds a PhD in Ancient Chinese Literature from Renmin University, Beijing.

Zhang is noted for her dramatic exploration of adolescent fantasies. Her stories are filled with violence and brutality, as well as love and passion. Her novel *Shi Niao* (誓鸟) was named the Best Saga Novel 2006. Her other awards include the Chinese Press Most Promising New Talent Award (2005), the Spring Literature Prize (2006), and the 'Mao-Tai Cup' People's Literature Prize (2008). In 2012, she was named by Taiwan's Unitas magazine as one of the top 20 writers under 40. She has been the chief editor of Newriting since 2008.

## Selected Works

NOVELS

*Shi Niao* 誓鸟 (2006). Translated by Jeremy Tiang as *The Promise Bird* (Math Paper Press, 2012)

SHORT STORY COLLECTIONS

*Shi Ai* 十爱 (2004). Translated by Jeremy Tiang as *Ten Loves* (Math Paper Press, 2013)

MG

# ZHENG WENGUANG

郑文光 [(1929–2003)]

Born in Vietnam to ethnic Chinese parents, Zheng Wenguang is often regarded as 'the founding father of Chinese science fiction'. By presenting it as a way of teaching popular science, he gained it official approval and a degree of respectability which as imaginative fiction it had previously lacked. He was also notable for championing its potential as a realist lens.

Zheng started publishing his science fiction writing in the 1950s, after moving to China in 1947 and completing a degree in astronomy at Sun Yat-sen University in Guangzhou. His novel *Flying to Sagittarius* (飞向人马座), released in the latter half of his career during China's second wave of science fiction in the eighties, is considered a milestone work in the genre.

## Selected Works

SHORT STORIES

*Diqiu de Jingxiang* 地球的镜像 (Shanghai Literature, 1980). Translated by Sun Liang as 'The Mirror Image of the Earth', in *The*

*Penguin World Omnibus of Science Fiction* (Penguin Books, 1986) and *Science Fiction* from China (Præger Publishers, 1989)

TH

314

# ZHENG XIAOQIONG

郑小琼 (1980– )

Originally from Sichuan, Zheng Xiaoqiong did several different jobs before getting noticed as a poet. Her poetry stands out for its cold and direct way of describing the poor working conditions of nurses and factory workers, and she has gained a reputation for a pessimistic and blunt outlook.

Zheng Xiaoqiong first achieved fame when she won the Liqun Literature Award from *Peoples' Literature* in 2007. Her style draws on classical Chinese literature, philosophy, and history, making some of her work difficult to categorise.

## Selected Works

COLLECTIONS

*Chuanyue Xingsu de Zhenkong* 穿越星宿的针孔, Translated by Eleanor Goodman as *A Needle Hole Through the Constellations* (The Chinese University Press, 2019)

REC

315

穿越星宿的針孔
鄭小瓊
**A NEEDLE HOLE
THROUGH THE
CONSTELLATIONS**
ZHENG
XIAOQIONG

# ZHU WEN
## 朱文 (1967– )

Trained as an electrical engineer, Zhu Wen worked in a thermal power plant for five years before turning to writing full time. He began by writing short stories, and later moved on to novellas and novels. Zhu's satirical representation of the brutal realities of a changing China in the 1990s turned him into a representative voice of his generation. One of his best-known works is the novella *I Love Dollars* (我爱美元), which was a runaway success.

Zhu Wen is also a filmmaker. In 2001, he released his debut feature film *Seafood* (海鲜), which won the Grand Jury prize at the Venice Film Festival. His second film, *South of the Clouds* (雲的南方) was awarded the NETPAC Prize at the Berlin Film Festival in 2004.

## Selected Works

NOVELLAS

*Wo Ai Meiyuan* 我愛美元 (1994). Translated by Julia Lovell as *I Love Dollars and Other Stories about China* (Columbia University Press, 2007)

Milton Keynes UK
Ingram Content Group UK Ltd.
UKHW011401060224
437323UK00010B/96

9 781399 910545